AGENTS OF CHANGE

*Practical Tools For Changing
Thoughts, Behaviors and Emotions*

By

Kurt-Edouard Neubauer

PRESS

Agents Of Change
by Kurt-Edouard Neubauer

Printed in the United States of America

ISBN 1-594676-79-8

www.xulonpress.com

ACKNOWLEDGEMENTS

First and foremost, I would like to thank God for grace and mercy and promising to make all things work together for good (Romans 8:28). Thank you for not striking me with lightning each time I've sinned (again) or made another faux pas (blunder). Mom, Elfriede Sprenger, and Dad, Edmund (deceased now these 11 years) - you supported me in so many ways, even when you didn't understand or agree. I can still see the pride in your eyes, Dad, when I graduated from seminary. Metaphors for concepts and feelings come easily to me - I believe in great part this comes from your "paying" me a penny a page, for what I read in that thick volume of sermon illustrations. You wanted me to stay out of trouble. Heidi Steimel - my sister (oldest child) - you have been there for me through so many times. I don't know how I'd have made it without you. Martin (middle child) and Lynette Neubauer- thank you for providing the place in Florida to write. It is lovely and I feel blessed.

To my children - Markus and Lukas and Mikaela: Thank you for putting up with me and my idiosyncrasies - especially my metaphors and mixed metaphors (diapers in the fridge - my metaphor for past events and feelings we don't want to deal with). I am blessed, for my fear had been payback (you know - a parent saying, "I hope your kids....."). All three of you together, weren't half the effort I was for my parents. You're great! I love you. Thanks for helping me with the technology Markus and Lukas.

Thank you Suzanne. You have been my friend for many years and through many trials. To all who showed me love as best you could, when I was often unable to take it in - thank you for trying. Lisa, Mici and Tanya - I don't know how you survived God's process of teaching me. No, the process is far from over. Thanks also to Kym and Terri - you keep me straight in my many hours of driving. Many others come to mind.

To my many teachers, professors, counselors: bless you. You saw potential and a future, when I only saw a juvenile delinquent and failure. Mrs. Miller (junior high substitute teacher), you had faith that I should work with people, because you saw empathy within me, when I was stuck in anger, rage and hopelessness. Together with my colleagues at the Pastoral Counseling and Education Center (Dallas, Texas), as well as the Dallas Society for Bioenergetic Analysis - everyone helped me get to the place I am today, with a greater balance of practical and intellectual grace and mercy. Thanks to Eleanor Greenlea - you asked me, "Are you ready to be seen."

To my many clients/patients: thank you for what you have taught me. No one will be referred to specifically in this book. I value confidentiality too much and respect your privacy. I will talk or write in the first person - I or me - which may strike some readers differently (more about this later). Thank you for pushing me to write.

Colonel Samuel L. Marks - Thank you for accepting me and utilizing my abilities and not feeling threatened. I don't know where I would be today were it not for you.

Finally, I wish to Sylvia Burleigh, at Xulon Press for answering my questions and encouraging me to complete my writing.

To anyone I have ever harmed, hurt or offended: Please forgive me. I am sorry.

FOREWORD

"The only thing that is inevitable, is change - unless it's from a vending machine." (from the internet). Change here is very ironic. In high school, we had a large computer - the sort that took punched paper tape. I decided I would never need these things, and here I am writing a book on a computer. Why another book? I resisted writing for many years because of this question. As Dr. John Hannah (Dallas Theological Seminary) said, "I don't want to rearrange sources and footnotes, just to write a book." Ecclesiastes 12:12 says, "There's no end to the publishing of books..." I also did not want a book to be about my ego. People from various walks of life have been telling me to write for years. Not until the last year, where I have had clients ask me to write, to have an adjunct to therapy, has the impetus come. The final straw was my eyes. Those who know my love of books, which has been lifelong, have been surprised to know I have been unable to read more than a few pages at a time in the last year. The metaphor finally hit me. I cannot see anymore. No, I don't think it's glaucoma or cataracts - I just can't take in any more. Until I am able to write and get out what is inside, there just isn't room for anymore.

An agent is a powerful force, that has the ability to produce an effect, in this case - change. "How many therapists does it take to change a light bulb? One. And the light bulb has got to want to change and get off the couch." Furthermore, so many self-help books have been written. Why this book? I have read many helpful professional and self-books, as well as theological works related to thoughts or beliefs, emotions and behavior. I don't wish to replicate anyone else's work, experience or insight; nor do I believe in plagiarism. I refer you to books dealing with specific topics, that I have found helpful. These authors don't know I have done this, some books may be out of print, some views I may not totally agree with, and I find these the best books I know on these topics, whether the author is Christian or not. Clients have asked for honesty, authenticity, and down to earth practical help. They don't want to mess around. I want to shoot straight. Here I offer you some agents of change.

I owe much to those who have gone before: none of whom are perfect, as I am not. No, I don't have it all together. Sanctification, the process of becoming Christ-like, is a life-long endeavor. I do not want to heap shame or guilt on anyone. We are where we are and who we are. If you or I want to change, then the question I am so often asked is, "How?" This book is not a substitute for therapy or your personal relationship with God. Our wounding in life occurs in a context of relationship to others: parents, siblings, classmates, spouses, etc. Healing, I believe, also happens in the context of a safe relationship, which can be therapy, good friends, and many other settings. I want this to be a pithy usable toolbox, out of which you can choose tools to help you live and relate in a healthier way.

Those who have gone before includes my history. As a therapist, I look at least four generations of a client's family, to better understand where they're coming from. This is never to blame, rather to discover what these generations before me have planted in my garden. When something sprouts, then I can know whether to weed it out or fertilize it and nurture it.

It is interesting to see how God uses things we might consider bad, for good. I start my history with Catherine II (Catherine the Great), who some 200 years ago, opened Russian controlled areas to her fellow Germans. Both my parents' ancestors were among those. My father was born in Poland after WWI, my mother a few years later in what was Romania, then part of the Soviet Union, now the Moldavian Republic (north of the Black Sea). After Hitler invaded Poland, my father was drafted into the German army as a Morse Code operator, was a British POW for 4 1/2 years after WWII ended (1 1/2 years in Egypt - 3 years on Cyprus). He was released to Germany, where he became a licensed tailor. After Hitler invaded Romania, my mother's family was relocated (yup, they were told, tomorrow you're moving, pack what you can) to what is now the northeast corner of Austria. She was in boarding school in what became East Germany, when WWII ended, and was fortunate to get out to northern West Germany, where she had heard her family was. My parents met, married, and immigrated to the United States, where six weeks later, my sister was born. My father later went to school, he'd only received a 4th grade education prior, and became a pastor/minister. Our parents raised us speaking German and we learned English from other children and in school. I have spoken German to my children, whether they liked it or not (I am powerless over whether anyone likes me).

Many of those who have gone before, for me, include: Sigmund Freud, Carl Jung, Wilhelm Reich, Alexander Lowen, Albert Ellis, Fritz Perls, Carl Whitaker and the many masters of Family Systems (for which I owe gratitude to Dr. Tom Parker, for instilling a foundation in me). I am grateful for the many authors and theorists who have helped me develop my own eclectic style. Carl Whitaker helped learn to listen to and trust the spirit within me, when I am being with a client. This was part of my process in learning to love myself, since love expels fear (I John 4:18). My hope and prayer is that this book will be practical and useful. My belief is that God is The Master Therapist and the Bible contains many truths about many things, including Philosophy, Sociology and Psychology. It doesn't directly refer to computers, cars, electricity and many other things I use, so I have learned to think for myself on these matters. They can be handy tools, and cars, computers and other electric items are known to be used for good and evil.

Who is this book for? Well, there is that overused word, dysfunctional. Since Adam and Eve, we have all grown up with less than perfect parents or families - in the best of circumstances. No one, had perfect families, including me. This is not to say that your family is all messed up. I don't believe in comparing families or blaming parents. I don't believe it is helpful to compare where I am to where someone else is - all that tends to happen is: someone ends up feeling < (less than) or > (greater than). I have no interest in saying, "You are a victim, because of your mom or dad." At the same time, Jesus said only those who recognize their need of healing will seek it (Matthew 9:12). If you are reading this, I hear you want change in your life, so this is for you. Notice, Jesus never forced anyone to be healed. They either asked Him or He asked them if they wanted to be healed. Pretty respectful guy.

I will make no attempt to make this book scholarly or politically correct. There are enough of both of those, so I simply want to offer something you can use daily, in addition to your own spiritual disciplines. I have not included a glossary, in spite of Jason's excellent suggestion, rather have chosen to explain words I thought would need definitions. Feel free to keep a dictionary at hand if you run across a word you don't understand. All it means, is there's a word you may not understand. It doesn't say anything else about you or me. (Using a dictionary was a discipline I learned as a child - my brother and sister were both valedictorians and told me to look up words. I am thankful now. Me? I didn't plan to live that long. I didn't think I'd make it to 18.)

There are many versions of the Bible. I am using Eugene H. Peterson's, "The Message//Remix," unless otherwise indicated. NIV refers to New International Version and KJV refers to King James Version. I will not always list a scripture reference. I encourage you to check in your preferred version, to see what it says, and to verify that I am not attempting to deceive you or pull one over on you. We do need to test the spirits (I John 4:1, "My dear friends, don't believe everything you hear. Carefully weigh and examine what people tell you. Not everyone who talks about God comes from God. There are a lot of lying preachers loose in the world.). The best book, other than the Bible, I know at the moment is "Seeing the Unseen," by Joe Beam.

If you are unfamiliar with how a Bible is set up, usually in the front, there is an index, which usually breaks down the 66 books (if you're not using a Catholic version) into Old and New Testaments. Some Bible's have an alphabetical index of the 66 books, most have them broken down into the order the books are placed in, whether in the Old (the first section) or the New (last section). It's like section one and two of a book. The Old Testament consists of 39 books and the New Testament has 27 books. You can look for where the book I refer to is located, and then for example 4:3, would mean, chapter 4, verse 3. Some books of the Bible have either a 1 or 2 or 3; I or II or III (Roman numerals) in front of them, which just means: first or second or third John or Samuel - whichever book it is.

My education is in Theology, Psychology and Sociology, and to me they are not mutually exclusive, for God is the source of truth, whether I recognize it or not. I don't see a separation of sacred or secular, and see these disciplines as integrated. Since I don't see a separation of sacred and secular, I will not always list a Scripture reference, because to me God's word is a part of everything I think about. I understand some people have been hurt by some practicing therapy/counseling, as well as some "ministering." This violation of trusting, hurting souls grieves me greatly. I am sorry for those of you abused by clergy or therapists. By integrating these disciplines, which should have never been divorced from each other in the first place, I seek to further the healing in our world through letting the Father of all wisdom into the process. Certainly God has granted insight and knowledge to others who do not exactly believe as you do or as I do. I am not intending to criticize or castigate anyone. I do want you to be able to discern in your daily life.

This book will not totally cover any specific area or topic. There are tons of books out there and many of them have helpful things. I only want to present certain things I know you can use. I will refer you to other sources, for there are many helpful books out there. I see no need to rewrite or plagiarize another helpful author's work. As I said above, check out what you read. Is it true? Does it violate what you know God wants you to do or not do? I rarely agree with everything in any book, so I don't expect you to agree with everything in this one, nor in any other book I suggest for further insight or expanded reading.

When I refer someone to a Twelve Step group (like Alcoholics Anonymous), I tell them to go six times, at least, to see what they resonate with, if there is something helpful.. As you read here, ask God to show you what is helpful, what is there you can use in your life. Read for yourself, not your partner or anyone else. If you decide you think someone else would benefit from what I have written, please get them their own copy. I have chosen to self-publish, so sure I wouldn't mind recouping my cost. My point here is, when I read for myself, I may underline or highlight parts significant to me. If I know I will give this book to someone close to me, either they may think I was underlining or highlighting to send them a message (no I can't control what they think, and I can avoid unnecessary problems); or I may actually read with them in mind and try to emphasize what I think God wants them to know. I prefer to apply what I hear to others, rather than myself or prefer to look for errors in spelling, grammar, etc. Be aware when this temptation comes, because it can indicate that you are getting close to something God wants you to deal with. It could also mean you find this book boring and need to do something else.

Some of what you read can stew in your mind's crockpot. It may be a seed that germinates at a later time.

I ask you to focus on you and what you are able to understand about yourself. What goes on in your heart, mind and body? What does God want to help you with? As Samuel Clemens (Mark Twain) is supposed to have said, "It's not what I don't understand about the Bible, that bothers me. It's what I do understand." If there is something this book helps you to deal with, great. If something doesn't seem helpful, put it in the crockpot and let it simmer. Also, I may not have said something in a clear helpful way. Don't assume it is all about you. Also don't assume it's all about me. It could be both.

Some clients or patients of therapy (I will use client from here on out), have felt invalidated by some therapists (I will use therapist as a term for psychotherapist, counselor - there are many disciplines who practice therapy. This includes Licensed Professional Counselors, Social Workers, Psychoanalysts, some Psychiatrists[today most Psychiatrists are responsible for prescribing medication, rather than performing Psychotherapy], Marriage and Family Therapists, Pastoral Counselors, and Psychologists[again, this discipline today tends to perform more Psychological testing, rather than therapy] - some may experience this explanation differently. I desire to clarify, and not place anyone in a negative category. There are other titles and licenses which I may have unintentionally omitted, for which I apologize. While I'm apologizing - any typos are my fault, not the publishers or anyone else.). What I mean by invalidation is: you have a particular religious belief system (I am not going to talk about being spiritual versus religious), and experience the therapist as trying to get you to change your theology or denomination. In the past the experience may have been that being religious was portrayed as being dysfunctional. This is regrettable, and actually would be a boundary violation.

When you go to shop for a therapist, yes, you may decide to use someone your insurance tells you you must use, or you may choose to invest money as you see fit. It takes a lot of courage to call a therapist - even more to actually go see her or him - even more to stay in the process. Ask other people you trust who they think could be a good fit for your personality and situation - no therapist is an expert on every issue and may still be able to help you. You can interview, over the phone and ask whether your belief systems are the same as your potential therapist's. This is a boundary you may set. You will never find another human who 100% believes exactly as you do. A good therapist will not attempt to get you to believe what he or she believes. Good resources are: AAPC.org (American Association of Pastoral Counselors) - they are "faith inclusive"; or AACC.org (American Association of Christian Counselors)- who tend to be more Evangelical - which is different than evangelistic. Also check out Samaritan Counseling Centers - they tend to be affiliated with the AAPC and be a good resource for sliding scale therapy (a reduced fee based on your household income). Many insurance companies will refer you to a therapist who identifies themselves as a Christian counselor. I have encountered some who call themselves a Christian counselor, who are more New Age. Another clarification: Most Pastoral Counselors I have encountered will say they are a counselor who is Christian, and would not say they are a Christian Counselor. If this is of concern to you, ask for clarification. You are the consumer - "let the buyer beware." All of this may not be of concern for you. The concepts of this book can work for you, no matter what brand of religion or belief system you ascribe to. If you want to know how to become a Christian, call 1.800.633.3446.

So, enough forward. Forward!
June 2004
Navarre Beach, Florida

CHAPTER ONE

"Words kill, words give life;
they're either poison or fruit—you choose."
Proverbs 18:21

Words Are My Reality

I do not mean that my words are reality in the way of objective truth. What I do mean, is that what I believe or think comes out in my words, behavior and feelings (I will use feelings and emotions interchangeably). This then, what I believe or think to be true, is how I will live and act. For instance, if I say that I believe that people will take advantage of me, then I will live in a way that is consistent with this belief. I will act toward others as if they are going to take advantage of me and will invite this sort of behavior. This does not mean that I made someone act that way, I just expect it. Anything that does not fit through the schematic or matrix with which I look at the world, I will interpret so that the behavior or words match what I believe. An example of this is, if I think people or certain people are critical, then, when they ask me where I got my hair cut, I will assume they are being sarcastic or critical, rather than simply wondering at which barber shop or salon I got my hair cut. (More about projection in chapter 2.) Eventually I learn to say, "Some people I have met are......," rather than "People are......." This subtile change lets people closer and judges others less.

Whatever the exact figures are, I don't know. What I have heard, is that about 7% of communication is the actual words I use, roughly 55% is my body language, so inflection or tone of voice must equal 38%. I often ask couples to not look at each other while they're talking, at least at first, so that they're not triggering off each other's body language. Written notes or emails can help reduce reactivity - clients often will bring in emails they've received or intend to send, and we work through them to not invite a fight.

Assume: when I assume, I make a fool of myself. Why you ask? Because I assume I know what you mean. As so often happens, I say, "You are implying that my haircut is....." The true statement would be, "I am inferring that you are making fun of my haircut." I cannot know what you are implying, only you can know that. Unfortunately, I hear something, and when I click on that word with my mouse, my hard drive goes to a file I have inside. Within nanoseconds, my library of words, body language and inflection (tone of voice) file inside of me says, "This is what this word means." Well, from my experience, this is what I have experienced this word means and that you also mean the same thing. This leads to misunderstandings and reactions. Furthermore, my reactions are connected to my hurts in life. I will say much more about reactions later.

How do I stop reacting to what someone else says? Well, there is something I can learn. This is called reflective listening, sometimes called mirroring or active listening. I tell you what I heard you say, not what I think about what you said, nor what I think you should have said. I use my own words, so I minimize sounding like a tape recorder or a parrot. "You're wondering who cut my hair?" I am listening to understand, rather than trying to attack or defend myself. I understand that whether you grew up in the house next door, or come from the same family, or same church or town or county or state or country or nationality or race, words can mean something different to different people. When I accept this as a fact of life, then I know that you are not purposely trying to say things to be difficult (and at times we may say things to try to irritate someone). I don't expect you to understand me or me to understand you automatically. I understand that we will understand each other better if I listen to understand, rather than trying to get someone to think or believe the way I do. Understanding is not the same thing as agreement. I can hear you and understand you, without needing to think or believe as you do.

Reflective listening is a discipline. The words I have used are not terribly complicated. Putting them into daily practice takes time. Give yourself the grace and mercy of a learning curve. A learning curve, is when I am learning spelling or writing for the first time and I have not had the time to practice. I will not be adept or accomplished yet, because I have just become aware of something I didn't know how to do before. I don't expect a child who was just introduced to algebra to be able to know and do everything well right away. Practice makes better. I prefer "practice makes better" because sometimes "practice makes perfect" can invite me to be critical or judgemental of myself. I don't need more guilt. By verbalizing my feelings I promote relief and clarity.

I add "yet" or "up till now" and "so far" to many sentences. "I am not accomplished at .... yet." "I did not know about reflective listening up till now." This way, I don't judge myself or you. I just didn't know about this before. Ignorance simply means "I do not yet know." I use grace as meaning something good I don't deserve. Grace is when someone tips my eldest far and above 15-20% (he is a waiter). Mercy is not receiving a consequence or punishment for something I have actually done. This is when the officer gives me a warning ticket, rather than a fine. I don't mean this grace or mercy to be permission or license for deliberately doing something I already know about.

As I use "yet," "up till now," reflective listening or any of the concepts I have yet to introduce, in time I will change. I will be less critical of myself and then others. Where I have been unable to take in love, accept love or compliments, I will begin to receive more. I will be able to accept more from God. This is a process, living a day at a time. As I practice changing my words, my behavior, thoughts and emotions will change. I will empower myself to live in the identity God has for me. Why do I need power? Because I see myself as weak, or at the mercy of others - fearing the future (usually resulting in depression or anxiety, because I "know" what is going to happen in the future, based on the past) or beating myself up about the past (usually resulting in depression, hopelessness).

Victim

No one is condemned to repeat the past, unless of course I don't learn from my past. Does this make me a victim of the past? I don't believe anyone has to be a victim of anything. (A great book that drives this home is Victor Frankl's "Man's Search For Meaning.") I used to say "I have a choice, unless someone puts a gun to my head." I now realize I still have a choice. When I say, "I don't have a choice," or "I have to," some form of the word "have" or must or should, I am feeling like a victim. Usually, we speak in all or nothing language (black and white thinking). In most situations, I have more choices than I am aware of. Brainstorming, thinking of all possible options or choices, without analyzing how successful a choice would be, is a way of getting as many options on the table, before deciding what is best. Would I want to live under a bridge? No, and this is an option. When I leave myself open to thinking about as many options as possible, I give myself the blessing of thinking more openly.

By recognizing that I am using victim language, I can begin to change my self-image and claim my Godgiven identity. God does not want me to feel like a victim. God is not the author of fear or confusion. In the beginning, I can hear myself saying, "up till now, I thought I had to.....and now I am learning I have choices." Romans 12:1 talks about changing our thinking. This is reprogramming my mind, my Operating System (OS). Paul talks about how we used to be this way (I Corinthians 6:11). My old passport had stamps from different countries Satan wanted me to visit. Now, I have a new passport, and I don't "have to" have those stamps in my new passport. My new citizenship is being crucified with Christ. I don't "have to" do anything for God. That's right. As I learn to listen to my words, and change them, I affect my thinking (more about that in the next chapter). While I respect (fear is often the word used for respect for God) God, I do what I do (being obedient, following God's laws[not suggestions]) because I love God. If I hang my head and whine, "I have to do what God says," then I let you know that I feel victimized by God. There is freedom in Christ. Can I do anything in my own strength? No, of course not. (More about behavior in chapter 6, more about victimization in chapter 4.) Again, this is all a process: sanctification on this earth is a process (While there are similarities to "self-actualization," they are not the same. Self-actualization is based on humanism and is about me making myself better. Sanctification is a God-driven process, with which I cooperate.).

And and But

And and but, are very basic words. We use them every day. There is an important theological truth with "and & but," as well as one about us human beings. But tends to negate either what comes before the but or what comes after. Think about it this way: "Today it is hot but cloudy" or "Today it is hot and cloudy" - both are true - hot and cloudy. But is so engrained in our language. Here is the theological application to "but & and": "God is merciful and full of grace and loving and just and holy and all-powerful and all-knowing and............" I see God (yes, this is just my feeble human way of understanding God - God is much more complex than I can ever imagine) as a diamond, with many facets. I can never see all the facets of a diamond with my naked eye at one moment. I cannot comprehend how God can be merciful and just and holy and loving all at the same time. I can't even find the words or metaphor to say how much He is on a different plane than I am as a human being. I just accept it. When Scripture speaks of God, there are many different facets. God made us in His image: male and female - God is portrayed with feminine and masculine qualities. God wants us to trust Him and He wants us to pray as the widow Jesus talked about in Luke 18:1-8. Before I pray, God is already answering. God also wants us to trust and have faith. - both are true. The Bible is the same. We may think there are contradictions and the truth is - "I don't understand God" or "I don't understand why the Bible (KJV) says to "answer a fool according to his folly when in the verse before it says don't" (Proverbs 26:4-5).

Well, as humans, I also see us as a diamond. I have many different facets. I do not necessarily see the different facets as mutually exclusive. "I know exercise is good for me and I don't exercise consistently." Who cannot say something similar? The point of "and" for me as a human is to become aware of the different facets of who I am. I cannot change something I am not aware of. In therapy, as I ask a client to speak with "and" rather than but, he or she hears themselves "giving a witness" to who they are. I further introduce another concept here, which is the speaking in first person: "I or me."

Why do I do this? Am I playing a controlling game? Is this just a matter of semantics? No. As I speak outloud, using I or me, with another person I have developed an intimate relationship (I am not using either "intimate" nor "relationship" with a context or meaning of some sexual act, as our society often erroneously does), I am "bearing witness" to who I am. This allows me to own my facets. "Huh, isn't that interesting. I say I'm a Christian and I drive over the speed limit." When I'm in a safe place, with someone who accepts me, I can recognize how my walk and talk may not agree and more easily change. On the other hand, when criticized or attacked, my human nature is to defend myself and change is quite unlikely. I believe each household should have a gallon jug of honey and a "to go" packet of vinegar on their table. Most people I've talked to, have experienced a "to go" packet of honey and a gallon of vinegar. This is about reaction and what we grew up with, which I will go into more, later. "I want you to speak kindly to me." "Hey! I was only being honest to you. You're such a baby, so touchy. No wonder I can't be intimate with you or get close to you." Much more about this later. Ephesians 4:15 (NIV) tells us to speak the truth in love. I don't have the right to throw up on anyone and then make it about them. So while I may be angry, how I say it makes a big difference. How did I get from the previous sentences to anger? Let me show you.

Anger

When I was in seminary, in Greek class, I was assigned the passage in Ephesians 4:25-27. How significant this was, did not hit me until after my next graduate degree (yes, Dr. Hannah - "death by degrees"). In the Greek, this is in the imperative tense, which means it's a command. "Be angry - yes, Kurt, be angry and don't sin. Don't hold onto anger overnight. Keep short accounts." When we deal with anger, we don't hold on to it and don't become bitter or resentful. In my experience, depression often results from held in anger. This is a form of emotional constipation. Physical constipation is painful, and while there can be many reasons for it, for this situation what is important to me is this: when I hold on to something and don't eliminate it from my life in a healthy way, it clogs up my life. Constipation results in toxicity - the body is being poisoned and it can be ugly, especially when others are affected by what's inside of us. Learning to eliminate anger or any feeling, is healthy. There's not a bottle of pills that forever solves this problem, because we may need to change our diet (food or what I watch or read or listen to) and exercise (being in touch with feelings and learning to appropriately get them out). This is a process and you're worth it - otherwise, the odor can be similar to that of those used diapers in the fridge.

Again, this is one facet of truth. If you were to take a concordance (A concordance let's me look up any word used in the Bible, to study a topic or word or to find a phrase I vaguely remember - like doing a word search on your computer. I'm using Strong's Concordance in this writing process - it's a Godsend.) and look up anger, you would discover many different facets of truth God has for us. Growing up, all I heard about anger was that it was bad. Christians shouldn't be angry. Yes, that has consequences. Remember, being intense or passionate about something, doesn't necessarily mean anger.

Some people internalize anger, and it attacks them spiritually, emotionally or physically. Others vomit onto others, venting - read this "just being honest." Neither extreme is helpful or healthy. I will address this more in chapter 5. So, how I got to anger. Passive-aggressive behavior can be seen through many different words or actions. Being facetious is making jokes, being witty, sometimes at the wrong time - I differentiate between being facetious and being sarcastic. Sarcasm comes from a Greek word, that means to tear flesh, as a dog would. Sarcasm is a bitter, cutting, caustic remark.

"Boy, traffic was really great today" for me is being facetious. "Nice outfit/suit, get dressed with the lights off?" is sarcastic. There are many different cuts we can make about a person's physical attributes or anything. They hurt. Sarcasm is passive-aggressive. It's like sticking a dagger in someone. When they say ouch, then twisting the knife and pulling it out. "What's the matter, can't you take a joke? I was just kidding. Man, you're touchy. You need to get thicker skin. I can't talk to you cuz you take everything so personal!" What's so insidious or treacherous about sarcasm, is being able to cut someone down, then making it all about them when they're on the floor bleeding. When you hear yourself being sarcastic, ask yourself, "What could I be angry about?" In this way, I have a chance to look at myself, apologize and change. There's a time to speak and a time to be quiet. Time outs aren't just for children.

When a quarterback gets up to the line and looks over the defense and realizes that he wasn't ready for what he's seeing, while he was in the huddle, and doesn't have an audible to call, that's the time for a time out. There's no shame in taking a time out. There's no honor in letting big lineman smearing you from one side of the field to the other. Proverbs and James both talk about our words. Again, it's a process. I can't do anything about what I've done up till now. I can ask for forgiveness, use duct tape on my mouth and learn to change.

Ok, so what am I supposed to do differently? Well, by becoming aware of what's going on inside of me, I give myself a chance to change my words. Maybe in the beginning, just being aware that I've made a fool of myself is progress. In time, I become aware that I'm in the middle of making a fool of myself and I stop myself. Half a fool is better than making a total fool of myself. As I check out what's going on in me: In Dallas/Ft. Worth, where I live and work, I'm aware that if I'm angry or hungry, I should take care of myself before I drive. If my anger or appetite is unchecked and not taken care of, then chances of my ego getting hooked in traffic is greater, and aside from any weapons someone is carrying (not just guns, knives - could also be tire irons or bats or whatever is at hand), a one ton weapon, at least, is being driven. When I'm in touch with myself, then I tend to not put myself in situations, where I could get hurt.

Traffic is not the only situation where a time out is appropriate. I have come home before, where I knew, in the back of my mind, that I should not talk, because something was going on in myself. Later, after reacting, I realized that I need to listen to the Spirit in me, telling me to get apart and pray and deal with whatever was going on in me. This can also apply to interactions with our children or work or wherever.

Men, in our society, have traditionally been allowed the aforementioned anger, eating and sexual arousal, as feelings to be okay, or ok to be in touch with. Action movie heroes model these three areas. Rambo, however, never seems to own loneliness, tiredness, sadness, insecurity, fear, paranoia, sickness - our society seems to have divvied these feelings to women, and not allowed them the anger, eating and sexual arousal. Men tend to not be aware of their having cycles or hormones, unless they relate to sexuality. Thus, I believe both men and women have tended to paint life with incomplete pallettes. Both men and women would benefit from checking in daily where they stand in all these areas. This would help to have fewer reactions and misunderstandings. I use reaction as a default mode, not an actual choice. A response is a choice, "I am choosing to respond." In times of stress, I tend to default to reaction - unfortunately this is often based on something I have seen modeled and is unconscious or sub-conscious, rather than a conscious choice. When we go to family reunions or get-togethers, is a great time to be in tune with ourselves. It doesn't take us long to revert to childhood roles or patterns when we're around family.

While in times of stress, we also tend to revert to former addictions: can be almost anything, from reading, TV, food, substances, sex, shopping, prescription drugs (our sin is creative). In stressful times, we can draw near to God and healthy friends. Isolation feeds addiction and sets us up to backslide. If we do, confess, repent and move on. Satan prefers we take a whip and keep punishing ourselves and not avail ourselves of God's forgiveness. Please don't hear me saying this is permission to go out and sin ("I was sinking deep in sin, Wheee!").

"I Statements"

Over the past decades "I Statements" have been taught, as has "reflective listening" ("what I hear you saying...."). Some of my clients have learned about them in school. That's exciting for me! A couple could be in my office, "You're a jerk!" I ask for an "I Statement" - "I feel you're a jerk!" Well, actually we often use feel instead of think - as in "The White House feels we should...." That's another sermon. Nonetheless, "I think you're a jerk!" isn't any more helpful. "When you said....., I felt (sad, hurt, angry, etc.)." Believe me, these words are simple and not always easy to say. When I feel hurt, attacked, whatever - the last thing my human nature wants to do is be thinking and speaking the truth in love. I want to hurt you. I want to do anything rather than reveal myself - yes, that's why I don't want to talk about me and what I'm feeling. So often, we remember the Miranda Act, "Anything you say, can, and will be used against you." So, why would I want to let you know what's going on inside of me, when I fear you'll throw it in my face? "I Statements" are a way of inviting non-reactivity. I want intimacy and am afraid of exposing myself even more to more hurt. This is a double bind. (A great resource here - "Love Knots" by Lori Heyman Gordon. Do a search under used books.)

I can go to a victim place here very quickly - "I can't win for losing," "if it weren't for bad luck, I'd have no luck at all," "nobody loves me, everybody hates me, think I'll eat some worms." I'm going to get a plate of those wiggly, rubber worms, so that I can have a good laugh at myself, and not let myself feel like a victim. When I talk about me, "I Statement," I'm not talking about you. This lowers defensiveness, and invites openness. I talk about me, because you know what, I've got enough to do with what's on my plate, without looking over at yours. I can talk about my momma. You know what happens when I talk about your momma. When I talk about me, I give you an opportunity to get to know me, which can invite intimacy. When I talk about you and not myself, I tend to stiff arm you and not invite intimacy.

Beating Myself Up

I can learn to listen how I speak to or about myself. I also learn to listen to others and how they talk about me. Because I am teaching myself to love myself, I accept less and less how others see me. Yes, if one or two call me a donkey, I can blow it off - if three or four, I start shopping for a saddle. When the light comes on and I gain insight, I don't have to say, "Well, it's about time" or "It took me forever" or "I'm so stupid." I can say, "I'm glad I am learning and changing. I'm glad I know this now and now it's helping me." There are many subtle ways I can change my words, which results in changed thinking and changed behavior. It takes many times of positive rehearsal of learned positive thoughts to counter the myriad of negative tapes I've had running in my mind. In addition, these words come with many daily mutations and variations, which run subconsciously, hundreds, if not thousands of time daily, until I become aware of their presence, and begin to alter them.

Defining or Labeling

My thanks to John McCormick, who worked hard on me to help me get this. That was almost 10 years ago, and the seed you planted has started growing. When I define you or label you, I'm telling you who you are. I know what your thoughts, feelings or motives are. This fits so well with the "I Statements." When I point at you, label or define you, I am pushing you away from me, and then I can further label you (more in chapter 4 on boundaries). "I know what you're thinking. You always.... or never...." (Ooh, more words I want to outlaw. I ask my clients to speak in first person, use and instead of but, and to never use always or never. Cute huh!). Here's what happens when I use always or never. It is human nature, you will naturally start thinking of at least one exception, and then I've lost you, because I'm not inviting listening or understanding, because I'm not listening. I'm telling you who you are, instead of trying to get to know you. So, yes, I believe not using always or never is helpful. At the same time, I believe we need to become bilingual. What I mean by this is, I can also learn that when someone uses always or never, they are emphasizing a point. Like when my mother used to say, "I've told you a million times to....., or not to...." Again, I offer both perspectives as ways to reduce reactions.

Another perverse part of defining or labeling, is when you tell me, "I'm not open to being defined or labeled" and I continue, then when you take care of yourself by leaving, I can try again by saying, "See, you're such a wimp, you always run. You're just a chicken."

Reactions

Why reactions, in a chapter on words? I kept trying to avoid this until later. When I react, I am coming out of that part of the brain that involves: fight, fright, flight or freeze (feeling paralyzed - deer in the headlights). It is often called the reptilian part of the brain, - the lowest functioning part. This is pure reaction - no holds barred, hitting below the belt. Here, there is no thinking. It's a badger backed in a corner. I don't think I have any options - it's a life and death perception - survival. A few months back, at church, a young man came up from behind me, put his arm around my neck and I flipped him onto his back. He meant it in fun and did not know my childhood. On my part, it was pure reaction. I wasn't angry. He could not have known. He does now. This part of us is where our boundary violations occured and I will say more in the chapters on the body and boundaries.

Another part of the brain is called the mammalian part, which is where we have the capacity for humor and nurture. Sarcasm doesn't come out of the mammalian part, rather the reptilian part. If you saw "Jurassic Park," what reptiles act like should be clear. Read James 4:1-2, or the book of Judges, or "Lord of the Flies" or just watch the evening news (if you can keep yourself from getting depressed).

The highest functioning part of the brain, for this discussion, is called the neo-cortex. Here we find rational thinking. In our relationships with God and humans, I believe we do best when we can access our neo-cortex, as well as the mammalian part of the brain. I can listen, because I'm not reacting - being defensive, shut down, isolating, attacking, in my addiction. I can be free to be who God has called me to be, rather than reacting or acting (when I act, I'm not being real, and can discount how people respond to me, because "If they only knew the real me," "they're just being nice," "I really pulled one over on them"), because I'm stuck in fear and playing a role - my false self can dissipate, melt away and I can be real, authentic. Everything I'm talking about is to help be less reactive and instead offer nurture and love, which come from the two higher parts of us.

Would or Could

Men and women are different (obviously not all men are the same, nor all women the same - my statements here are intended to be generalizations). Many would say, "Viva les differences!" I heard a song on the radio that talked about men only being good for propagation of the species. I understand the pain. I know there are different agendas in the world, have been since the Garden of Eden. I also ran across a website about "no marriage" - there is a lot of pain there as well. I see the pain from men and women every day. For those who wish to understand and learn how to deal with life co-ed, learning to be bilingual helps. Dr. Deborah Tannen has written a number of enlightening books on differences, "That's Not What I Meant," "You Just Don't Understand." Dr. John Gray's "Men Are From Mars, Women Are From Venus" series has been popular.

In my experience, until a man becomes bilingual, don't ask him "could or can you do....." Men tend to hear this as about ability, rather than a request. For some reason or other, we tend to hear this as an affront, rather than "would you do this?" In addition, men tend to need a more direct question, or else they don't hear they've actually been asked to do something. Women tend to hear direct statements as rude.

Questions

Women tend to ask questions and feel uncared about when not asked questions. Often they expect men to be their girlfriend and don't understand that he doesn't ask her more questions, "Any caring person would know to ask more questions, don't you care?"

He shuts down, because he feels labeled or defined, "You're not good enough, you don't do it right," is the message he hears. When he hears questions, he feels like he's 13 or however old, and mommy is trying to pry information or interrogate. He feels invaded or violated and he shuts down. Men usually ask questions to get an answer. If they want help, they will talk about a problem. They often have trouble understanding why a woman would talk about a problem, and then not take his advice. He's frustrated she ignored him, "Why did she ask, if she was just gonna blow me off?" She's frustrated because, "He didn't listen, rather he gave me advice!" Again, learning to be bilingual is important. He may ask a yes/no question and be frustrated when he gets an answer longer than yes or no.

Well, it has been my observation, that about 90% of questions avoid making a statement about one's self. Instead of telling you, "I want to go to Wendy's," I say, "What do think about going to Wendy's?" When you tell me you want to go somewhere else, I haven't risked as much. I also may be angry that we aren't at Wendy's. If I don't know how to ask, that's another issue. The truth is, I can avoid intimacy by asking a question, because I haven't said what I want. You don't get to know me as well, because I can always say something to not own what I want. I can also stay inside with my hurt, because I didn't feel heard. I can ask what you think about the President, rather than tell you what I think. This is safe and at the same time, does not further intimacy and understanding between two people. Try this out - listen to others when they talk - when they ask a question, is it truly a question, or is it a statement of some sort. Reflective listening can help sort out this confusion. I don't have to tell others their questions are actually statements, the point is to realize how this process works, and be able to choose how I communicate.

Asking Questions Differently

The world is not going to come to an end, unless I think it will - which then becomes my reality and you won't be able to tell me differently - if there are misunderstandings. The learning curve process can help us here. Does this mean I should never ask questions? Again, there can be a male/female difference. Women tend to think making a direct statement is rude and often experience men as rude when they do. Men tend to experience women as being "wishy washy" or "beating around the bush." Who is right? Well, I'm a man, so what do you do with what I say? I can only tell you from experience, that the more explicit I am about what I want or need, the greater the possibility I will get more of my needs met. Again, learning to be bilingual helps and I can utilize reflective listening to help clarify and understand. This is not about cross-examination as a lawyer does in court. The lawyer is not attempting to understand. He or she is wanting to prove a point and set up testimony in a way that will win the case. If you communicate as a lawyer does in court, with others, you will not invite intimacy. The legal communication way is about control.

In Matthew 7:7-11, Jesus says to ask. In context this is with God. It is equally true, that if I don't know what to ask for, I can no more ask God for something, than another human being. I have experienced, that in many families, the 12th Commandment was, "Thou shalt not ask for what you want!" Why the 12th, well, because often the 11th Commandment was, "Thou shalt not want at all!" If this was true, then how could we ask God or another human for what we want? If I believe I won't receive anyhow, however I got there, I either won't ask, or I will ask in a way that invites another person to not give. In addition, if I learned I would not receive, I tend to be attracted to someone who knows how to not give. It is a dance we learn so young.

So, in order to change, I can write a list: "I want:......." I may write down 20 things or 120. I don't analyze or criticize anything. I can write another list later of the things I heard in my head, whoever's voice it may be, where I told myself "I shouldn't want this." This doesn't mean I am going to get everything I want. However, if I learn what I want, then I can learn to ask. God will teach me about motives in the process. Some families have some unwritten rules, which affect everything I'm talking about: don't think for yourself, don't talk about what's really going on (we have secrets), don't trust, and don't feel (either don't feel what you're feeling or don't feel what you're feeling and you're responsible to take care of everyone else's feelings). This seems to be true in many sorts of families, with variations. (Adult Children of Alcoholic groups talk about this.) As I work through my past - my baggage, then I am able to be less reactive and then more able to give and receive love. When we aren't able to talk about what's really going on, we have secrets, skeletons in the closet and denial. Denial is when we keep stepping in elephant droppings and say there's not an elephant. Elephant droppings are a fairly good clue that there's an elephant somewhere nearby. Owning this truth, allows me to change, or else every time I open my refrigerator, I am surprized that it smells like dirty diapers. Getting out of denial helps me love myself and others. God knows anyhow, and many others see our pain or baggage anyhow, because, we're not as great at acting as we think we are. Remember the "childrens'" book, "The Emperor's New Clothes?" Just because you get out of denial, and say the emperor's not wearing any clothes, doesn't mean everyone or anyone is going to thank you saying "blessed art thou." You also don't have a right to go knocking others out of their denial. Take care of your own stuff. The only exception I see is in Matthew 18:15-20. Part of why we were put on the earth is to give and receive love. This is true in our relationship with God as well as others.

When I go into a fast-food restaurant and they ask me what I want, I don't expect them to guess. I'm an adult. I can ask for what I want on my burger or what I don't want on there. They are okay with me asking for what I want. Babies aren't able to verbalize what they need. We learn to check their diaper, or know by their tone of voice, whether they're hungry, tired, sick, need to be held or need their diaper changed. This process of learning can take time. As an adult, as I learn what I want, learn better ways to ask, and then involve myself with people who are able and willing to give, then I receive more.

Why?

Ok, here's another word I want to ban. Yes, it's verboten (forbidden - sorry, German was my first language - yes, my

German-Englisch dictionary is next to me as I write. Sometimes words come to me in German.). The sports ad says, "Why ask why?" I agree. I've checked with people whose first language is other than English, and this concept seems to be present in a number of cultures. When asked "Why?" another reaction occurs: defensiveness, feeling like a child, where a parent is asking, "Why is your room messy?," "Why were you 10 minutes late?," "Why weren't your grades better?," "Why can't you be like.......?" The concept includes the connotation of, "You're wrong, you better have a good answer, it doesn't matter what you're answer is, it's wrong, and you still better answer and not have an attitude!" Ouch! I have discovered that asking, in the fashion of Detective Columbo (no pun intended), "Could you help me understand? I don't understand." This is best done in your best, "Pass the potatoes please" voice (unless of course that was shouted). "Would you help me understand?" is a valid question, as long as I'm not thinking, "You're wrong and I'm gonna prove it."

Passive or Active Tense

No, I wasn't an English major and I'm very aware of how we speak. You want change, right? Ok, when I use passive tense it can sound like: "That happened to me" instead of "I did that." "We had an argument" instead of "I argued." There are many ways we speak in the passive tense rather than in the active tense. "A good time was had" rather than, "I had a good time." When I speak in the active tense, I will own my own responsibility for my life and actions. When I speak in the passive tense, I will feel more like a victim, like something happened to me. Active tense helps me own my agency - my being an active force, being capable of action. I don't want to blame anyone, I want to change. I use the active tense and become aware of my own responsibility for my thoughts and actions. Nobody makes me feel or think or do anything.

Other People's Words

Other people's words can be powerful in my life. If someone

says, "You scare me!," I learn to listen. I may remind them of someone from their past. (When you have a reaction to someone, ask yourself, "Who do they physically remind me of? Does their behavior remind me of someone from my past or another part of my life?" Could there be something about me that I need to look at? Certainly, my beard or hair may trigger something in them. The true statement would be, "I am scared when I see your hair or beard or whatever." "I feel intimidated," "I don't trust you." We tend to hear the "you" and not the statement, "It is hard for me to trust." Of course, if I have lied or cheated, you would be wise to be cautious. Remember, it is difficult to risk showing who I am and making the satement about myself, "It is hard for me to trust, or I am afraid."

I am learning to not take other peoples' words personally - this is freedom. The truth sets you free, first it'll tick you off, then it'll set you free.

Beating Myself Up

I can learn to listen how I speak to myself or about myself. I also learn to listen to others and how they talk about me. Because I am becoming more aware of words and wanting to understand, I don't automatically take everything as Gospel.

Deflecting

Deflecting is a defense mechanism, designed to not let others get close to me. I may change the subject, tell a joke, switch TV channels, leave the room, or start a fight. I may intellectualize (talk to not feel - resulting in isolation), project (see something in others that bothers me, when it's actually a part of me), become obtuse (where I appear to not understand or am ignorant), or engage in obfuscation (where I muddy the waters, make my thoughts or the conversation at hand cloudy or confusing). As I become aware of protecting myself in these ways, I can look at renewing my mind, and letting others close to me.

CHAPTER TWO

"If God can use Balaam's donkey, He can use me."

"When I was a child, I talked like a child,
I thought like a child, I reasoned like a child. When I became a
man, I put childish ways behind me." (I Corinthians 13: 11, NIV)

Renewing Your Mind

Why is my mind so important, if I want to change my life? School textbook and curriculum authors, TV show and movie script writers, owners of media all know the answer to this. Whoever controls the mind the soonest, controls the person. "That Hideous Strength," the third volume of C.S. Lewis's space trilogy explains this concept well. Ask yourself, "Why is this being written, why at this time?" I can be a thinking person. Try this exercise: Tell yourself 20 times outloud, "I am weak and can't do it." Then outloud say, "I am strong and can do it!"

Well, at the most basic level - "It's not what happened to you or what you've experienced - it's how and what you think about these experiences that determines the meaning of the experiences." A colleague of mine, Julie Welwood, says, "When I see a vehicle barreling down on me in my rear-view mirror or tail-gating me, I tell myself they have a wounded pet in their lap and they're racing to get to the vet, to save its life." She gets out of their way and drives peacefully on. If I tell myself, "What a jerk, I'll show him!," then my action is a reaction rather than a response as Julie chooses. Not only will my mind get into a yucky place for quite a while, I probably will pass on my attitude to others for the next bit of time. I have choices about how I think about life's experiences.

Sometimes, I can just tell myself, "Don't sweat it - the world won't come to an end." Certainly in traffic, the seconds I shave off my drive time, I also shave off my life with the added stress. As I learn to change my thinking, making a paradigm shift, I give myself more options. I think about myself differently. How I think - who am I? "You're not who you think you are; you're not who others think you are; you're who you think others think you are." It doesn't have to be this way, because this means I am giving others power over me. First of all, I don't know what others think. Secondly, what I project onto others is about me. Thirdly, when I think I know what you think about me, I'm reacting to a phantom or straw man which says a lot about me, and nothing about you. I am giving up who I am, probably don't even know who I am, and then can get angry at you because you don't "let" me be me. I will feel like a victim. When I feel like a victim, I will naturally want to victimize you, because you did it to me. While we know the Golden Rule, "Do unto others as you want them to do unto you," often what is true is either, "Do unto others as they have done unto you," or "Do unto others as was done to you growing up." This is about self-esteem. I believe self-esteem comes from doing what I esteem or believe is important. When I do what I value and know to be right, I don't need to deal with guilt or feeling ashamed and will have self-esteem. I cannot get self-esteem from you, for that would be borrowed esteem, which can be taken away.

When I grasp this concept, I can grieve what was done to me, and change my thinking. "Love your neighbor as yourself," says this in another way. The intent of Jesus' second greatest commandment is to be loving toward others - it's proscriptive. Unfortunately, my observation is that this also is in fact, descriptive. Here's what I mean - "I do love others the way I love myself," and it's not always pretty. I do need to learn to love myself, and learn to take in God's love or others' love. Now, I don't mean this in a narcissistic or self-centered way. "You deserve a break today." What do I deserve? As you see or read or hear advertising, be aware of how it violates the 1st and 10th commandments. Have no other gods before you - idolatry, is often the theme of advertising, along with coveting what my neighbor has or how my neighbor looks. (Some times, a workout gym and its mirrors can be a temple of idolatry of the body.) A book I have found helpful, that recommends reasonable minutes of time daily, as well as healthy eating is, "Body-for-Life," by Bill Phillips.

Often, the words I use reveal how I think about myself and whether or not I love myself or others. My words can reveal how I was treated growing up. If I am critical of others, finding fault, correcting them on their dress, grammar or any other mannerism (for their own good of course), trying to change who they are, I in reality am letting them know that I was not accepted for who I was/am. I am pushing them away, all the while saying I want people to be close to me. Think of it this way (I don't say, "Try to think of it this way," because it's as Yoda said, "There is no try, there is only do."): What I get, is what I wanted. How can that be? I didn't want a speeding ticket or want to gain weight or get in debt or whatever. Well, when I make declarations of my intentions - you know, New Year's Resolutions - I am saying this is what I claim to be wanting or wanting to try to do (oops, here's the try again). "I ostensibly want to lose 10 pounds this year." On December 31st, I know what my actual or de facto goals were. I wanted to gain 10 pounds, because I sat and watched a gazillion hours of TV and ate unhealthy food and didn't exercise. I pushed the accelerator and ignored the speed limit. My belief may be, "I want what I want and I want it now." This will bring consequences. Read Romans 1:18-32 and you will see examples of such choices. You may have your own example. Are there exceptions? Certainly. I'm not judging you. Perhaps you lost your job and debt was unavoidable. My point is, when I own what I have done - then I can learn to change my thinking. When I sit down with the donuts, I can say, "I want to put on weight." You may be tired of my saying this is a process - and it's a process. In time, I can say, "This donut is not my friend, it's poison and will harm me." I will feel badly about myself when I don't take care of myself. I may enjoy what I'm about to buy, and will I pay interest on interest for this brief feeling?

When I do what I've done, up till now, I will continue receiving what I have received, up till now. That's why I want to change, because I don't like what I've received or experienced. At least that's what I tell myself or others. There is no magic wand - no quick fix. Loving myself is saying no to myself, when what my ego or childish (different from childlike) or sinful part screams for. Saying "No" to my children or another person, can be loving, no matter what they say ("I hate you because you won't let me drink, smoke or play with the butcher knife" - part of becoming bilingual is being able to hear that sometimes, when someone says, "I hate you," it's an expression of "I'm angry" and I can learn to hear the anger whether someone owns it or not). I can't control their reactions or responses, and while they may attempt to define me, I am not required to take the file label they offer me and stick it on my forehead. Again, I want to be able to utilize my neo-cortex - I want to respond, have choices and make my own decisions, because when I think I'm a victim, I can be pretty pitiful.

My self-care is improved by my thinking. My thought may be, "If I do or don't do this, they will be angry or will withhold affection or conversation." A true "I" statement is, "I am afraid I will feel lonely, or sad or whatever, and I cannot control his or her reaction. I can feel - I won't die if I feel sad or lonely or afraid. I can do hard things" (thank you Betty Thompson). At the same time, perhaps my fear is valid. A great resource is Gavin de Becker's "The Gift of Fear." He writes of learning to trust your instincts (gut) in situations, where I might say, I am learning to listen to the Holy Spirit's prompting. If you read "The Gift of Fear" and have issues of sexual or physical abuse, please keep your feet on the floor, breathe in a way that allows your tummy to go out or up. This will allow you to stay grounded (much more about this in the chapter on the body). I have had someone come back and thank me for suggesting this book, for they passed it on, and it literally saved someone's life. I believe every woman should read "The Gift of Fear," and every man as well.

Please remember, "You can change imperfectly." Think of it this way: 1) at first, until I become aware of something, I do it imperfectly; 2) once I become aware, I do it imperfectly until I start changing, 3) then I think about things as I am doing them better, and 4) it becomes a habit and I'm not always thinking about it. An example of this is: Driving a car is something I don't know how to do, until someone teaches me. Of course, I may need to unlearn some things I observed from others. When I'm learning, whether in driver's education or however, I consciously think about adjusting mirrors and seat. After a while, I have practiced and it becomes my second-nature. I believe I am going to be at various stages of this process throughout my life. This is grace and mercy. It is like the progessive tense in the Greek of the New Testament. It is a process.

Have you ever experienced the following? "They did something little or insignificant, and suddenly I realized I had overreacted." What is happening here? What I see happening is, it's like looking at a computer screen, seeing a small symbol that says "today's date." I click on it and suddenly find myself having reacted and saying, "My reaction was much greater than that little symbol." I see this as God giving me a blessing. My reaction comes in less than a second, and I may initially feel like a fool and I am learning to change. When I click on that symbol, my hard drive and operating system interact and ask, "What kind of file are you calling up?" My hard drive pulls up a queue or stack of files that are related in some way. My reaction is to the cumulative value of the stack of files. These files have emotional memories and my reaction is to a lot of past, unresolved files or issues. God is saying, "Here's something I think you're ready to deal with, so you can put the past behind you and press on to your higher calling." Initially, this probably won't feel like a blessing. One client told me, "I didn't want to deal with my issues and was angry at you for seeing them and asking me to look at them. I'm glad now." No, it's not easy. It can be painful and takes time. Well, how did these files get created?

When I walk around a corner and encounter someone I wasn't expecting to be there, I get startled. What I may initially say is, "You scared me!." I hold my breath - you know the startle reflex - and a file gets created. When I create a file, I may or may not remember it. It just gets filed away, my computer does what I tell it to do, that's just the way it works. My computer doesn't care. It doesn't pop up a window that says, "Breathe and talk this through!," until I teach my mind to do this, like the above doing things imperfectly. (Yes, I have had problems with computers.) Unintentionally being startled is very innocuous (innocent or harmless). Someone may intend to scare me. Most of us have done this and/or experienced this. As I learn, I learn to say, "I startled," because it is a true statement about me. This reduces my reactivity. I don't want to give you power over me, you probably don't even want the power - it's all in my mind, which is what I see as reality or truth. When we encounter other things in life: being teased, bullied, emotionally abused or neglected, physically or sexually abused - these things happen at a developmentally young age, a part of our development gets arrested or stopped. That's why, when I react I seem like I'm a child - I go back to reacting like I did when I experienced something hurtful or harmful. In times of stress, I lisp in my mother tongue - a client was in a stressful place and began speaking in the dialect they grew up in.

Now, I am learning to breathe, talk about myself and take back the authority for my life, which God wants me to have. By the way, this talking about myself is not, saying anything and everything that crosses the conveyer belt of my mind. It is not a monologue, where I only talk about myself and don't listen to you. I will say much more about this later. When I breathe and feel grounded, I learn to be strong in the Lord, not blown around by the wind. As I become more grounded, I can more easily work through my childhood files, where my defences were not yet developed. Think of it this way: A parent says, "You make me angry!" Is this true? No! The true statement is, "When you said (or didn't say) or did (or didn't do) this, I felt angry." This is important, because then I'm not making you responsible for my feelings. They're mine. God gave them to me, just like a dashboard has gauges. They let me know something is going on that I need to be aware of. Sometimes the feeling lets me know that my thinking is out of whack. When I'm angry, I feel like someone crossed my boundaries. Is the feeling valid? Yes, and perhaps as I own my feelings, respond rather than react, I become aware that it was how I was thinking about the situation that brought me to anger. Anger isn't always necessary.

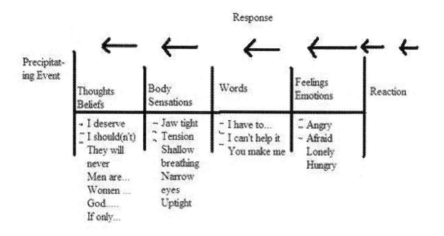

Looking at the above graphic, at the right side you see a reaction. Initially, I am oblivious to or unaware of my patterns and reactions. In time, as I become aware of my reactions, I am able to think and realize that my reaction is to something, which I will call a Precipitating Event (on the far left). If I'm yelling, upset, shaking a fist in traffic, then the precipitating event would be the car being driven into the space in front of my car. Now, I am beginning to have a chance at change. In this process, as mentioned in the previous chapter, I can make less of a fool of myself. This begins to open up the possibility of my responding. It may be, that initially I become aware of my feelings or emotions in this process. In the traffic example, I can become aware of my words or gestures, and realize that I'm feeling angry or afraid. I fear I might have a wreck. That makes sense in this situation.

I may become aware of my body sensations: breathing changes, heart rate, skin temperature, jaw tight, eyes narrowed, tension, balled fists. These would be consistent with my feelings. My words are probably consistent with what I'm feeling and what's going on in my body. I have no control over the precipitating event. I can control my reaction and words, moreso as I progress in this process. I don't need to control my body sensations or emotions - they are alerting me to a situation in which I want to take charge. The body sensations, words I hear myself using, feelings and reactions, are all gauges on the dashboard of my life. I don't put duct tape over my gas gauge or hit the gauge with a hammer and shout, "Don't you ever show me you're empty again!" My gas gauge is useful - it's my friend. My anger and fear and loneliness and other emotions are my Godgiven friends - to teach me, not to stay stuck in them. Fear enslaves.

Where I find the meat and potatoes (sorry if those aren't in your diet), is my thoughts and beliefs about the precipitating event. As I begin to become aware of my thoughts and beliefs about the precipitating event, I see that some of my thoughts and beliefs can be consciously known. "No one should pull in front of me that close or without turn signals and if they do they're a jerk (or whatever sanctified language goes on in my head). If I'm not aware of my thinking, I will keep thinking as I have up till now, and continue experiencing life as I have up till now. I probably have cognitive distortion - my thinking is distorted. AA talks about "stinkin thinkin." Much of our thinking, until we become aware and start making changes, has non sequiturs. This is a Latin phrase meaning that our conclusions don't logically follow. "I just saw a black truck - all trucks are black," "a woman or girl rejected me in the past, all women will reject me, I need a man instead of a woman," "my father died when I was young, therefore men will abandon me and so I need a woman." The possibilities are endless, and also self-defeating. By the way, as an adult, I cannot be abandoned - when I feel abandoned as an adult, I am wrestling with a younger part of myself.

Up till now, so far, yet - these are God's grace and mercy. Bill Gothard had those button's "PBPGINFWMY" (please be patient God is not finished with me yet). Amen! As I own my thoughts and beliefs, without shaming or beating myself up, I take my thoughts captive and give God control over them. Some of my thoughts and beliefs, may be beyond my conscious awareness. I can discover some of them through extrapolation (estimate or infer) - if I act offended, then I must have a thought similar to..... "This feels offensive or unfair!" I don't have to get my thought exactly right. I think about how old I felt in my reaction, and can figure out how I probably thought at a certain age. This will get me close enough. Some of my thoughts and beliefs come from an early age. We encountered life from the moment of birth - whether you define this as conception or delivery. We make decisions about life, God, work, men, women, marriage, etc., from a very young age. These are the earliest lines of our program. We don't think every thought consciously, no more than we think "To turn left, I must push down the turn signal" or "to accelerate, I must push down my right foot." Once we've done something long enough, it's a habit - a default mode. Habits can be helpful or harmful. This part of changing my life is like rehabilitation. I may not need to do physical therapy forever. It's a change, takes time, can be painful and I can do it. No one comes out of being in the hospital for months in a body cast and then runs in a marathon tomorrow.

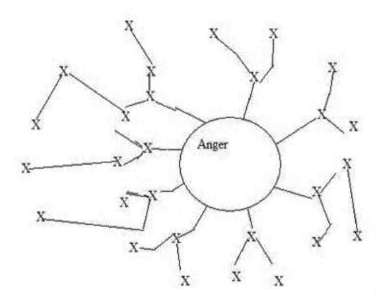

Here is an exercise, which I call a web (often ends up looking like a web) my clients have found helpful. It is a brain storming exercise - an experiment. You can't do it right or wrong. No one has ever brought their homework back (yes, I assign homework - I don't decide whether anyone decides to do it or not - those who do the homework report it being helpful.) and it looked identical to anyone else's. Just like my first illustration, dealing with precipitating events and reactions, you can utilize this for any situation. Ideally, you would be alone, so you're not concerned about anyone else interrupting your process, or invading your privacy. If at all possible, set aside (allot) as big a block of time as possible, so you don't cut short (truncate) your process. A table or other large, flat surface helps to not poke holes in the paper, if that bothers you.

Take a large piece of paper (this helps provide the space to be open to more words) and in the middle draw an imperfect or perfect circle, it doesn't matter. In the middle, write the word you want to explore about yourself. This may be anger or any other emotion, a person, an issue in your life, like God, mom, dad, sex, anything. Draw a line from the circle and write the first word(s) that come to mind. This may be where I have placed an X, or however you decide to do this. Another word may come to mind that connects to the previous word, or perhaps a whole different branch of thinking. There's no right or wrong here. You write as quickly as words come to mind, without worrying about "how will it look?" or spelling or penmanship. Do not analyze "Why did "ice cream" and "doggy doodoo" come to mind. Being concerned about spelling, penmanship, sentence structure or analyzing can greatly hinder or inhibit your experiment. You write until no more words come to mind - there is no maximum number of words, where you must stop yourself. It is helpful to have at least 10 words or entries. Again, no one has ever come back to my office with the exact same number of words. For this exercise, don't censor your words. Lines may be straight or curved or you may not use lines at all. When absolutely no more words come, you are done with the first part of this exercise.

The second part of the exercise is to take another piece of paper, perhaps lined, and take each entry or word(s) and let a sentence come with that word in the sentence. Don't try to make a sentence, just let it happen. You will have as many sentences as you had entries. Ok, now you're done and wondering why I've asked you to do this exercise. This is a way of finding out my thoughts and beliefs about precipitating events or anything that is of concern for me. It is a way of skirting your defenses and finding out important information - explore, become aware and then open up possibility for change. I have no desire to knock out your defenses or you would be defenseless. Imagine 300+ pound football players. Would you rather run at them or around them. The web exercise is doing an end around play on your defenses. If you ever decide your defenses don't help you, you will change them. This exercise helps you find out information which your defenses might not allow you to otherwise discover. It's a way of respecting and honoring your defenses.

Some of the information you discover you will say, "I already knew this about myself.," or "At some level, I knew this, now it's more concrete," or "Ouch! I didn't want to know I think or feel this way.," or "Where did this come from?," "I will have to think about this one," "Hmmmm," "I wouldn't want anyone or everyone to know this!" or you may just scratch your head, or chin and wonder. It's information. I will never have all the information there is to be had about anything. I can decide when I will make a decision with as much information as possible. What I am not aware of, is in my blind spot and can ambush me. (Check out johari.com for more on blind spots.)

I don't shame myself for my thoughts or beliefs. They just are. Once I become aware of them, I can change them. I don't need to change them all. I need to decide whether my thoughts or beliefs are consistent with God's word. If I believe, "If it doesn't work out, he or she is the wrong one and God will forgive me - no biggie," then I go to God's Word and see if this is true. If my thoughts contradict God's Word, then I need to submit to the Master Programmer and change those lines of programming. If my thought or belief is: "Look both ways before crossing the street," hmm, guess I could keep that one. "Spend less than you make." That's a keeper. By the way [btw], "It's not what you earn, it's what you save." (Thank you Richard Frederiksen, Ph.D.) Financial discipline brings freedom, as discipline brings a freedom. Asking myself, "Can I live without this in a crisis?," also helps me take care of myself. Is this something I truly need to buy, or am I giving up my financial freedom, by spending this money now? Will this end up in a garage sale? What am I feeling? Am I wanting to feel something else and that's why I'm buying this - so I will feel something different, or not feel what I'm feeling right now. (More about this below.) Since some of my beliefs came at an early age, obviously my logic was that of a child at that age. Telling a five year old, "You think like a child," doesn't make sense. Of course a five year old isn't going to think as an adult would. "Huh, it makes sense I would have thought like that, and now that I'm an adult, I can decide how I want to think or believe and move on."

I work to have a choice about how I think. I decide whether to continue thinking as my tribe or family taught me - whether to continue believing what the media/TV or school presented. That is always my decision. I can be aware of my emotions and body sensations - I don't have to kick or hit or be verbally abusive. I change my thoughts and beliefs, isn't that beautiful - I'm not condemned to continue as I thought, up till now. My body sensations and emotions will follow suit. They will become consistent with my newly chosen thoughts and beliefs over time. Now, I can learn to think, be in my neo-cortex, have choices and options, love myself by giving myself a time-out and bless others, rather than sharing a curse. This is one way to reverse the curse of previous generations' choices.

While we say, "There's no fool, like an old fool," "can't teach an old dog new tricks," "can't change a leopard's spots," God is full of grace and mercy and can change even me. "A word to the wise" is something a wise person needs to hear, and won't be offended for being told so. A fool's ego gets defensive and has closed ears. One way to change your thinking is to read the book of Proverbs every month, changing the version of the Bible you use monthly, if possible. With 31 chapters, it's possible to read the chapter that matches the day of the month, and get through every month. A different version may get through your defenses more easily, than a version you've been using for a while. Familiarity breeds contempt and sometimes we can't see the forest for the trees.

It is helpful to understand logic, because often I can have a failure in logic. A great resource here is: "Practical Logic - An Antidote for Uncritical Thinking" by Soccio and Barry. This will help you discern when you listen to yourself, others and especially sales pitches. At the same time, it's not all about logic. Sometimes I won't understand and can hold this tension or anxiety about not having "the" answer - God is not the "answer man" - trust God and don't be concerned about the answer. Job waited a long time and got some answers - I don't read that he got all of them. David was annointed king many years before he actually sat on the throne.

CHAPTER THREE

"Know them by their fruit - trust them to be who they are - and pray for change."

"Life is like a cafeteria - eat only what belongs on your plate."
(Forrest Freud - Kurt's nom de plume)

OPA (Other People's Anonymous)

What? You've never heard of this 12-Step group? No, it doesn't exist, although I refer many people to this very helpful group, I've joined it myself. What does it mean? Well, in AA (Alcoholics Anonymous), the first of the 12 steps is recognizing and owning/believing, "I am powerless over alcohol." In OPA, I recognize, "I am powerless over other people." Why is this important? God has not called me to get other people to change or be a certain way. Other people don't need to be my higher power. A man or woman or child makes a lousy higher power. This is a form of idolatry. While this may seem severe, consider the following: A spouse does something to please their partner. If this is done with pure motives, in other words, without expectation, then the giving partner is not giving to get. I am giving because I love. If I become resentful, it is probably from one of three things: If I do something you didn't ask me to do, you could have done yourself, or I really didn't want to do it, in this case, I have attempted to disempower you, or be the knight in shining armor. If you could have done it yourself, I'm not doing you any favors. If you didn't ask me to do it, perhaps we have a game going on, which is a negative thing. It's no fun having a game, where the hook gets stuck in your mouth. I have choices and so do you. I'm not responsible for you and I can't make you or anyone happy. No one can make anyone happy, no matter what any song or movie says (intimacy also doesn't develop in two hours).

If I'm not happy, it's because of my relationship with myself and my relationship with God. I have expectations (thoughts and beliefs) which are not helpful. Are there valid expectations in marriage? As adults, whether at work or in relationships, we have a contract. It is ok to have some expectations. The more explicit a contract is, the clearer the agreement. While some ceremonies may be called "shotgun weddings," we still have a choice. When we enter an agreement, vows are a contract before God and church or family, we decide this is a contract we make. If we're not happy in this one, as the saying goes, "Wherever you go, there You are." I take me wherever I go. If I don't change, I will be who I have been. In order to be in a relationship, I must explore myself, become aware of myself, accept who I am, love myself, and change what I can.

The other side of this is, I also must accept other people. We all want to be accepted. If I'm walking the aisle, thinking you'll be different, then I'm planning a subtle form of manipulation, and I don't accept you for who you are. If something about you bothers me now, it'll bother me more later. Neil Clark Warren, founder of www.eharmony.com, says it well when he talks about our "pickers being out of whack." We choose partners often based on wrong criteria, and expect this "Gift from God" to be someone they're not (pass the buck please - "the woman you gave me," Ok, Adam probably didn't have too many women to pick from). So, I accept someone to be who they have shown themselves to be, being honest with myself. This is not judging someone - this is being discriminating (being able to distinguish between different things). I want my children to be able to make wise choices. Accepting someone for who they are is only fair. I don't have to label someone, I simply observe and think and know what is negotiable and what is non-negotiable in my potential contract.

My favorite story is: One day, I woke up and realized I'd been sitting on a fire ant pile (If you've never encountered the actual ants, you're not missing anything. Just imagine the sting and burn.) I had about 550 bites. I realized that I didn't have to sit on the ant pile any longer, well, at least for today. The next day, I came back and after 500 bites, decided I'd had enough. I kept cutting back 50 bites a day, until one day I realized - "These are fire ants - they bite, sting and they always do!." I accepted them as they are. Right? The next day, I took my Bible and read to the fire ants, as I sat down. They converted. Nope, they bit me all they could. The next day I took my hymn book and sang old hymns and "praise" music. They still bit me. I realized I could take a crystal bowl of honey, and then they would love me and not bite me. No, it took me a long time to realize they are who they are. There aren't plush fire ant dolls. I don't need to go yell at the fire ants or curse them. I accept them now for who they are and look before I sit down. I am powerless over changing fire ants.

I don't go around gossiping about people I've experienced as fire ants. I learn people are who they are, I accept them and know God can change people and I'm not God and never will be. God can change even me. I can sing, "Just as I am." There, but for the grace of God go I. After I repeat, "I thank God I'm not like other people," and laugh at myself, I don't judge others. I can forgive them and I don't need to sit on the ant pile. You recognize a tree by the fruit it bears. It's not judging to say, "This is an apple tree. I don't want an apple. I will look for a pear tree." If someone else likes apples, great. That doesn't say anything about me. When someone else says, "You have to like apples, because I like apples. I will be sad, if you don't like apples, like I do," then look out. They may not be able to differentiate between themselves and another person. They need to know, when the snake in the "Jungle Book" movie says, "Trust in me," that they can distinguish between words and actions. "The check's in the mail."

We may have this type of fusion in our family, workplace, school or place of worship. Surgery to separate siamese twins is long and difficult - and not impossible. If you like Mexican food and don't like Chinese, well - OK. That doesn't say anything about you or me. It says nothing about me, that I like strong coffee or spicy foods, other than "I like strong coffee and spicy foods." You don't have to like what I like - I don't have to like what you like. It's not about me, when you like something different. That's why God made us as individuals. You may enjoy different books, movies, TV shows, vacation spots, sports teams, or whatever. I think that's super. You don't need to convince me I should think like you do. If you do try to change me or convince me that your preference is what I should want, I can listen, understand you and still know that I am who I am. I don't need to fight. I also can decide whether I want to spend time with you. If people don't want to be around me, I can look at what I do or say, and see whether there's a reason. If I always do, what I've always done, I will always get, what I've always gotten. When I keep doing what I've done, maybe I'm just verifying my research data - maybe I don't believe that what I've gotten is a result of what I've done. Maybe a true statement is, "I don't want people to be around me," or "This is what was done to me in the past, and up till now, I've been trying to get someone to understand what it was like for me, which is why I was doing it to them."

Progress is success - today, "I will change what I can, and accept what I can't." If I want to see someone I can change - I look in the mirror, when no one else is around. When something really irritates me in someone else, I have learned to look at myself, and ask myself, "Is this something I don't like and I do it myself? Maybe it's beyond my awareness, so far. God, help me know. "God, have merciful on me, I'm a sinner!" There's another group I want to create: Sinner's Anonymous - a place we can gather every Sunday morning, or whatever day you decide you will worship God. A place where anyone, since we're all sinners, can come for love and acceptance, not to continue in sin, rather where we get first aid, emergency care, long-term care - where the wounded are not executed.

When I understand that I cannot control anyone else, I can't make anyone like or love me, I can't make anyone respond to me in any particular way, then I am free. I look at the page labeled: What I can't control. Time I spend on this page is wasted time and energy. It is an exercise in futility. The other page is: What I can control. Throughout my day, I can ask myself: "Which page does this activity or time or person fall on?" This allows me to know my priorities and keep me from investing time and energy in something that is sure to not bring me dividends. At least no positive dividends will come from sinking energy and time in areas I have no control over. If I continue to spend my resources in something I have no control over, I can ask myself, "What's my payoff?" There is always a payoff. I may not initially identify what I'm getting. We do everything for a reason. Maybe, "I want to feel frustrated, overwhelmed or ..."

CHAPTER 4

"Just say yes or no. Just say what is true."
James 5:12

Boundaries

What are boundaries? Skin is a boundary. A fence is a boundary, as is a lock (helps keep honest people honest). (The best resource I know for learning this is: "Boundaries" by Cloud & Townsend.) Setting a boundary is dealing with the manure in my barn, not borrowing your manure and not welcoming your manure. You need your own manure, for it will fertilize your fields.

If I don't have boundaries, I don't respect myself, and I will invite people into my life who won't respect me or are unable to respect. I don't make people disrespect me. Just because I learn boundaries, does not mean anyone will rise up and "call me blessed." I don't depend on what others think or feel. Boundaries are for me. I don't set boundaries for others. When I begin to develop boundaries, others will have an adjustment period. If I have been a doormat, the one who has walked over me, will be able to find another to walk on. They may need to adjust, and if they choose to continue being who they have been up till now, they will find someone else to be their victim. I no longer feel the need to volunteer. Jesus didn't heal everyone, didn't hand out free lunches everyday or do a magic show every day. Did the people around Him like this? No, and he let them be who they were. He took care of

Himself and His disciples and even they weren't "happy" with all His decisions.

I need to be able to say, "No." Without a no, I don't have a yes. If I don't have a no, I risk becoming passive-aggressive - I may say yes, and do "No," all of which is unhealthy. Without a "No" I am a pushover. People need to be able to push against me and know that someone is there - that I can provide resistance. Imagine one extreme of someone with a Ph.D. in boundaries who treats you with respect, dignity, and doesn't violate your boundaries whether you have never heard of boundaries or couldn't spell boundaries or couldn't even appreciate their appropriateness. At the other extreme are psychopaths/sociopaths, some tele-marketers, some lawyers, some politicians, probably some of every category, who don't care whether you have a Ph.D. in boundaries - it is their intent to violate your boundaries and take advantage of you. Each extreme probably has 1% of the population in its membership. The other 98% of people having varying degrees of understanding and respect. As I learn more about boundaries, I will attract those who respect boundaries, and am less attracted to those who aren't able to respect boundaries. This too, is a process.

Try this with someone you trust: I do this with clients to help them understand respect and boundaries. Stand with your back to a wall and place one foot next to the wall. Ask the other person to push against your hands. Tell them this is not a contest, you are simply going to provide resistance and will take care of yourself (meaning, if you need a break, you will say so). If you are taller than they are, get down into your legs to be on their level. This is a chance for them "to be all they can be" (like the Army ad). Use both of your legs, simply to give yourself balance and strength. This isn't about winning. When someone pushes against me, and I take care of myself, I'm not a pushover. I can stand on my own two feet. I have backbone. You can trust me, when I tell you I will take care of myself and then do so. You also discover that when I take care of myself, you trust yourself to find out what's inside of you. You don't have to take care of me.

If someone can push me over, one of two things tends to happen: either they will hold back, not be all they can be and then whether consciously or unconsciously feel like the world is not safe. They can't trust or respect me, because in essence, I lied. I didn't take care of myself. They will treat me with kid gloves, walk on eggshells and not discover what they're capable of. They will pull back from contact with me. Children (they don't develop defenses and coping mechanisms) and those not yet able to understand the process will tend to think, "I'm too much," rather than "He's not able to stand up for himself." This is unfortunate, for there are long-term effects of this. The other danger is: When I don't stand up for myself, the other person goes into their reptilian brain and gets the piranha or shark gleam in their eye and either literally or figuratively go for the jugular. They also do not respect or trust me and at some level also know something is wrong, because I'm not being an adult. Our society has much damage from parents, adults, teachers, society not being respected and there not being consequences. We do our children a bigger favor by having boundaries and backbone, than trying to be their buddy.

On the other hand, if when someone pushes against me, I suddenly stop providing resistance and then attack them, another problem occurs. Again, the other person learns they cannot trust me and don't respect me. They may fear me, and learn to hold back, in order to feel safe. They can't be all they could be, and in order to feel safe, will treat me with kid gloves, walk on eggshells or withdraw. The world is not a safe place. This is what happens when someone is physically, sexually or verbally abused. Until we work through our experiences and get our thoughts right, we tend to find people either to do to them what was done to us, or to get them to do it to us. I don't have to label myself when I repeat a pattern in some way. Once I become aware of the pattern, I prayerfully find help, support and/or therapy and allow God to heal me.

Think of clothes: If my boundaries were crossed and I now have impaired boundaries, at one extreme I would be wearing fishnet. The other extreme is wearing concrete. Concrete is a barrier, fishnet is negative vulnerability. A middle place would be having a closet from which to choose different outfits. Sometimes I would wear cutoffs, other times long pants - short sleeved shirts or jacket. I can choose to wear something made of Gore-Tex, a material which keeps out wind and rain, while at the same time breathing and allowing sweat to escape. To me, reflective listening is being able - at times when I want to understand, not react and not allow someone closer to me - to wear a suit of Teflon, Kevlar (used for "bullet-proof" clothing, wall material, military helmets) and Asbestos. This allows me to very consciously know that what someone is saying is not about me. What they say, can bounce off or run off or reflect off.

Boundaries are necessary for good intimacy. Imagine you're on a bus headed from Miami to Seattle, sitting in the window seat, all places full, and the person next to you begins telling you every operation or romantic interest they've ever had. You've never met this person before and you start praying for the rapture to come right now. This is about boundaries. TMI (too much information) can be a big clue that someone has impaired boundaries. If this is a client, I want to help them secure their boundaries. In other facets of life, I may not have the invitation to help someone, nor the desire. This is a choice we all have.

Another situation is this: Visualize sitting on one side of a table with a stack of cards in front of you, on which are written everything about you. The least revealing thing is on top, the most revealing thing is on the bottom. Across the table from you is a person with their own stack of cards. You breath and decide to reveal your top card and wait to see if the other person can handle it or if they run screaming from the room. If they remain there and are breathing, they and you have sort of passed a test. You then wait for the other person to decide when they will flip over their top card. They too want to see whether you can handle their information. A healthy relationship, romantic or otherwise, can develop this way, with each person alternating self-revelation. This process takes time. A friend of 10 years takes, well 10 years. There are no short cuts. This is healthy. When we rush into any relationship, we tend to ignore red flags, and not respect ourselves.

Here are some red flags at the above table: One person turns over another person's card(s). This is a boundary violation and should cause alarm, at the least this should be talked through and respect re-established, if possible or desired. One person turns over too many cards at one time (TMI). Hmmm, again at least talk, because some-thing's going on here. One person starts pulling cards off the bottom of their stack. Talk any of these situations through and visit with good friends who aren't afraid to tell you like it is, or see a therapist who won't beat around the bush with you. Just like praying overnight before making a purchase decision, take your time. You decide whether you want to continue pursuing relationship with anyone. If you want some no nonsense material about how not to make foolish decisions, check out Dr. Laura Schlessinger's books. Listening to another's information reflectively, allows understanding, trust and intimacy to develop.

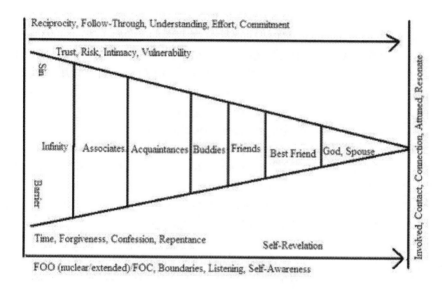

In this figure, starting at the left, in the middle, you see infinity. There is an infinite number of people I could meet. As time (bottom line) progresses, I begin to meet more people in my Family of Origin (FOO). As I get older, I decide who I spend time with - my Family of Choice (FOC). I learn more about boundaries. My FOO and FOC may overlap, for some they are one and the same. Others have no overlap. I decide and there are consequences either way. I have reasons why I decide what to do. I learn to not be a victim. During this time, I am meeting different people, developing relationships, which take time. The top line indicates reciprocity (mutual giving and receiving) which a healthy relationship needs. When there is reciprocity and follow-through, which allow me to develop trust. Trust, like forgiveness, is a choice. You can't make me trust you. I decide when I enter the process of trust. Trust is not a single place, I trust some people more than others. This is one side of the coin. Another side of the coin: I trust people who have acted in harmful ways, to be who they are. When I have more listening and under-standing, I am moving toward deeper relationship, where I reveal more of myself, I put more effort and commitment into my more inti-mate relationships. I will risk more. Throughout all of my movement, I am learning to have healthier boundaries. Intimacy develops, doesn't happen. Intimacy comes with positive vulnerability, where I risk. I don't over-risk. Those with whom I have the deepest connec-tions are also those I'm the most involved with and resonate with. I spend the most time with these people, where I share my self-aware-ness. Through time and working through difficult situations, I allow relationships to deepen. This process applies to how my relationship develops with God as well. As I practice forgiveness, confession and repentance, my relationships - with God or others - progress. When I hide my self, my sin, my hopes and fears and dreams, I put a wedge between myself and others. Intimacy cannot develop. When I sin against you and/or God, intimacy cannot develop until I confess and repent. I won't talk about salvation in this context.

My Values

I need to be aware of my own values, as well as another person's values. A Russian proverb says, "Don't look for a partner on the dance floor, look in the vegetable garden." Take your time to know your values. Don't settle or give up what is important to you. Do you want someone who is better than nothing? When I feel that desperate, I know it's time for me to take a time out, until I can get back into my neo-cortex. I sure wouldn't want someone coming up to me and saying, "Hey, you're better than nothing, wanna start a relationship?"

Boundaries are about many things. I didn't force my children to give hugs to anyone: relatives, acquaintances or strangers. Respect certainly can include a handshake. This may seem awkward or strange to you, maybe not - I have learned to say, "I would like a hug, are you open to a hug?" We never know who has experienced boundary violations, and for whom a hug can be traumatic. My suggested way of asking allows for another person to have dignity, respect and a choice. I want my children to know they can have some choices. Yes, I made them go to school.

Sometimes we tell our children, "Don't say no to me!," then chew them out when they don't say no to drugs, alcohol, sex, etc. I can listen to what my children are telling me, and still have a boundary. I can listen to understand what they want, I can talk about their interests, fantasies and dreams. I don't have to squash their ideas. I can listen to understand, I don't need to agree. I can ask them to talk about what it would be like if they had the Ferrari or made it to the big screen. When I say, "That's stupid. Few people accomplish that!," what I will accomplish is that my child, or whoever, will either withdraw from me and/or others, as well as not easily open up to me again.

Human nature includes many things, including going from one extreme to the other. I can recognize within myself or others, the following: trusting everyone (being naive), not trusting anyone, falling in love rather than taking time, touching without permission, not asking for what I want, receiving something I don't really want. Some times I will be balanced and live in moderation. Other times, while I am moving from my previous extreme, trying to find the middle ground, I will swing to the other side. My ultimate goal is to learn to set and maintain my boundaries and respect others' boundaries.

CHAPTER 5

"To be touched tells man that he is loved.
To touch tells man that he is lover.
Touching is therefore, being
Tango ergo sum!
I touch; therefore, I am!"
(Calvin Miller - "A Requiem For Love" p. 20)

Your Body

God made us with a body, mind and heart/soul. We know how we think and feel affects our body. We are all capable of becoming sick physically, by how we think and what we think about. I refer clients to Philippians chapter 4 to learn about gratitude and what to think about or meditate on. When I focus or think about or meditate on positive things, I will have the peace of God. Praise brings gratitude and gratitude brings praise. The feeling follows my thinking. This brings me health. Read Proverbs, you will discover many things you can do, and ways you can think differently to help your body.

As I am writing, I have become aware of a body issue. Food, the fuel I put in the body God gave me. Do you remember the "three Hebrew children?" Read Daniel chapter 1 and see where Daniel, Hananiah, Mishael, and Azariah ate only vegetables and drank water, and within 10 days looked healthier than those who ate the royal diet and had the best wines. I always heard this preached, that the point was they were faithful because of the king's food being connected with idols and so forth. Well, I'm wondering. Hmmm. I have looked at books about eating raw. Hallelujah Acres is a great resource, founded by Dr. George Malkmus, the author of "Why Christians Get Sick," which talks about our eating habits and the effect different things have on our bodies. Well, over the past week, I have been eating raw fruits and vegetables and having energy like never before. The one exception was eating a great burger and yummy fries, and I became drowsy. My mind is much clearer without the processed foods. Processed foods are talked about as "dead food." We have many ailments and who knows what those many words I can't even pronounce do to my body. I know with wheat, they take out the bran and germ, the most nutritious parts, and then throw back some processed things and sell us flour. Hmmm. I'm not saying you should go raw, just wondering out loud. Ezekiel Bread is a product based on the book of Ezekiel, and is supposed to be very healthy. Something to ponder.

Why do I talk about health and diet (I don't mean dieting, rather what we eat)? Well, when I am with a client, I am concerned for their whole being. I ask them to get an annual checkup. I also ask them to see a psychiatrist for any medication for depression or anxiety or whatever mental issue they are dealing with. I do this because, while a family physician can prescribe whatever she or he wishes, this is not their specialty. I wouldn't refer you to a psychiatrist for an annual physical or to prescribe antibiotics, because it's not their specialty. I care about the whole person. Ask other professionals you trust, which psychiatrist, if you have a choice, deals best with your situation. As in any profession, not everyone is an expert at everything.

Many of us feel shame about taking medication for depression or anxiety or even ADD (I have had feelings of shame here and have learned that if I needed vitamins or insulin, I wouldn't worry about what others think. So again, I joined Other People's Anonymous.) When there's a chemical imbalance, that's all it means. How I got there no longer matters. Getting back into balance now does matter. The whole person includes the body, in addition to the emotional and spiritual. We are more than emotions or thoughts carried around in a hard drive. Our bodies are important. Yes, one guarantee is that our body will die. It also is God's temple here on earth. Our bodies are not throwaway cups, they're crystal.

I have several years of training in a discipline called, "Bio-Energetics." Dr. Alexander Lowen, M.D., developed this under-standing about 50 years ago. His theory says we carry the history of our lives in our body. When someone touches a different place in our body, perhaps in massage therapy, we may remember an event from the past. When I hear a particular song, I can go back to a place in the past. When I smell something, I can remember a room or event from my youth. Read any of Lowen's books for a greater understanding. I will stick to my theme of practical change, and Lowen's books, as well as Bio-Energetic therapy are very powerful. I can talk about feelings and thoughts and make changes. My body carries my experiences, hurts and attitudes.

I talk about standing on my own two feet. My body can be explained in so many metaphors. When I can stand on my own two feet, I can be grounded. I will over-simplify and say that for me, grounding means being in touch with my feet, breathing where my diaphragm is relaxed, which allows my lungs to fully expand down-ward, which then will push my abdomen outward if I'm standing, or upward when I'm on my back. In addition, when I'm grounded, I can stay in eye contact with someone while breathing and in touch with whatever I'm standing on. If my head is in the clouds, I'm not in touch with the ground and not on my own two feet. If I'm zoned out, I'm not present - I'm not grounded. I have no desire to make my body my higher power - I don't want to get into idolatry. I want to change and live here on earth, while I'm here, rather than existing.

Another metaphor is "being uptight." When I'm uptight, I'm feeling tension, most specifically in the upper parts of my body - shoulders, neck and head. When I am uptight, I will be breathing shallowly from the upper chest. My diaphragm is not relaxed and I'm not in touch with my feet. Since I'm not fully breathing, my lungs don't fully extend downward, I'm not getting as much oxygen to my brain as possible and I'm not thinking as well as I might. When I get in a panicky place, feeling anxious, I tend to breathe shallowly and rapidly. If I'm hyperventilating, I'm not able to think clearly and am not in the present. Sometimes we say we're hyper. We tend to be fearing the future.

I believe God wants us to live in the present and not be in fear. Try this: hyperventilate and see what it feels like. Then lie on your back, with your knees up. As you inhale, let your tummy rise up and as you exhale allow your tummy to return down. This is how infants breathe, unless they experience a trauma that interferes and startle. When a client is relating a traumatic event, I ask them to keep both feet on the floor, breathe fully and stay in eye contact with me (not a staring contest). This allows them to breathe through the experience, not create another file, and begin to work through old files, which enable them to have less files to react with.

This also allows the brain to create new pathways for processing old experiences. Just as students walking across grass wear a path in a lawn, so too, when I think about an event, I keep thinking about it in the same way, which keeps me in a trance-like place. When I'm grounded, breathing and in eye contact, I can talk about an experience, rather than re-experiencing it. This protects clients and me from traumatization. This way a client can now see a video and not be in the video. (This information does not come from Bio-Energetics, rather is condensed from, "Trances People Live.") I know there is great controversy about hypnosis in the Christian community. All I care to say at this point is how I see us living in trances and what this looks like. I have no desire to encourage or dissuade you from hypnosis.

In some senses, hypnosis can be like any tool - it depends who is skilled and what they desire to accomplish. We are often in a trance: when I am reading a book and very much in the story, I am entranced. When I am driving on a long trip where the terrain is the same, we talk of highway hypnosis. When I am zoned out, I am in a trance. My point here is that when I am not able to change how I act, at the very least, I'm in a trance-like state. My goal is to get out of this condition. When I'm in a trance, I am not consciously in charge, my body is relaxed - that's why this is scarey. I suddenly realize I've driven 30 miles and don't remember any specific markers. This is dangerous whether I'm driving, or living daily in a trance. The point is to become alive, consciously choose to see and change.

Children seem to be able to pull this off better than adults. They see things we take for granted. This is part of what happens in going into trance: I become comfortable, relaxed and see things that I'm familiar with every day. It becomes a habit - we can exist zombie-like. I want to have choices and live, not exist. Status quo, unless it's healthy, is unacceptable. Every time a specific topic comes up, I don't want do argue, sigh and walk off. God loves us and wants us to change. If I am stuck in the window I have open on my computer screen, I want to work it through, close it and be able to open other windows God brings to my awareness. Being able to get a different perspective can bring about change, much like putting a different frame on a picture can enhance or change my perspective on the picture.

Pollution begets pollution. Garbage in, garbage out. The old computer phrase is true of our minds and bodies. What I put in, affects everything else. Why else would advertizers pay millions of dollars on short segments during a Super Bowl? They know advertizing works. The songs we hear, ads we see or hear, TV or movies we watch, books we read and food we eat all do something to or for us. 30 years ago, my mother said she'd heard about soap operas and decided to watch them. After a week or two, she said, "If you're not depressed before you watch them, you would be after."

Many physicians connect ADD/ADHD (Attention Deficit Disorder/Attention Deficit Hyperactivity Disorder) at least in part with diet (sugars, processed foods, food dyes, vitamin/mineral deficiencies). Doing the right thing, whether in my diet or thinking or behavior, is not always convenient. Sure feels better later. Disease prevention, whether mental, physical or spiritual, is less costly than treating disease (less cost: money, pain, hurt - to self and others). This is equally true for our society - bad policies come from not living right or well, which comes from not thinking well/right

CHAPTER 6

"Procrastination is waiting to feel like doing it."

Your Behavior

"Would you tell me, please, which way I ought to go from here?"
"That depends a good deal on where you want to get to," said the Cat.
"I don't much care where -" said Alice.
"Then it doesn't matter which way you go," said the Cat.
"- so long as I get somewhere," Alice added as an explanation.
"Oh, you're sure to do that," said the Cat,
"if only you walk long enough.'"
(Lewis Carroll, "Alice in Wonderland")

Behavior is interesting. How do we decide what to do? What is logical or common sense to me, may not be to you. Flip Wilson used to say, "The devil made me do it." Am I my higher power? Why am I alive? What is the purpose of my life? "The Purpose Driven Life," by Rick Warren, explains this well. "It's about God."

There is a principle called, "the point of diminishing returns." Imagine the best bakery inviting you to a sitting, where you may have as many pieces of the yummiest cakes and pies, for 5 cents a piece. That's right - a nickel. At this time in our world, that's only 1% to 5% of what you normally would be charged. Of course, I'm assuming you would eat sweets. You might not eat the day before, so you could take advantage of this offer and enjoy as many pieces as you might. The first piece would be exquisite - "Wow, only five cents!" At some point, you would say, "It's not worth it to eat another piece." That is the point of dimishing returns. Well, in life we reach a similar point, where our behavior does not get us what we say we want. Just like a hamster, I keep running in circles and getting to the same place. I am ready to do something different. This could be an accident or some other significant event that really gets my attention.

I want to change. Ok - Great - Super. Here is a warning. Why a warning? "My wife has wanted me to change for years" or "my husband has said he wanted me to change for eons." They will certainly be happy I finally got to this point, right? Well, years ago, Alcoholics Anonymous realized something that Systems Theorists have also realized: When there is change in a system, the system resists change and/or takes a while to adjust to the change, whether it's considered positive or negative change. Change brings stress, no matter what kind of change. AA realized when one person in the family stopped drinking, the other family members often would start acting in ways that the alcoholic would experience as, "We wish you would start drinking again. We said we wanted you to stop and now we don't know the rules. We used to be able to focus on you as the problem or scapegoat in our system. We saw you as the "bad guy/gal" and knew how to feel like a victim. Now who do we blame?" This is where the concept of codependency came from. The addiction or behavior in the system served a function - the others didn't need to change. Well, we all need to change, and when we do, we need to expect that others will have an adjustment period or phase. Just plan on it, and you won't be disappointed.

Imagine you are on a teeter-totter or seesaw. You are balanced with them (often called having equilibrium or homeostasis). Neither one of you is totally happy in the relationship and you decide to make a change for the better. That means you move and you create an imbalance. In order to have a new, healthier balance, the other person can decide to make a positive move. This is the best possible outcome. When I change, I must change because this is what I decided to do, out of love for God and myself. If I change, "Because he or she wanted me to," I will resent this other person, feel like a victim, and probably throw it back in their face at some point. This is not a positive transformation. This is an attempt to control the other person's feelings or behaviors. "I will do this because I don't want them to get or feel angry or I'm afraid they will leave me." This will not "work." I hear this often: "I have changed and it didn't work!" I understand this is frustrating. The point of my changing is not to get someone else to change. The point of my changing, is because I needed to change. I want to be a different or better person. Success is being who God has called me to be, not getting someone else to be who I think God wants them to be.

Okay, so I change for healthy reasons and give up trying to influence others. If others change, that can only be the sprinkles on top of the frosting of the cake. I am responsible for making the cake and the icing on top. My change may be an invitation to change. When I move and create the imbalance, I have the opportunity to deal with my discomfort, and I can leave you your discomfort. It can be hard to watch someone else in emotional pain. They may say things like, maybe we should get a divorce, or I'm not sure I like this. I can hear this and sit with my own anxiety and know that your anxiety is yours. I don't need to rescue you from your feelings and I can do hard things and take my anxiety to God. God doesn't always rescue us from painful situations. Sometimes, there's something we need to work through. God would truncate or cut short the process we need to be in. Hard times can develop patience, spiritual muscle and emotional endurance. God wants to make us strong, so He can use us on His team.

When I have moved on the seesaw, I understand you may move to have a new, more enjoyable balance or you may decide to jump off. I can't decide for you and God will help me through whether you change, which of course will mean I will need to adjust to your change (remember when there is change, I will have an adjustment period), or whether you jump off, or try to get me to go back to being the way I used to be. I help nothing by telling you what I think your motives are - I have enough to do with my own change, without focusing or worrying about you. I need God's grace and mercy as much as you do.

You know, there are some things in the Bible, I wish weren't there. For example, Ephesians 5:25-28 ought to say, "Husbands, love your wives if they respect you and take care of your needs," it doesn't say that. I believe that wives equally wish Ephesians 5:22-24 would say, "Wives, respect your husbands if he loves you as Christ loved the church and he's the epitome of spiritual leadership," it doesn't. In fact, here's one of the biggest things I don't like about the Bible: it never says, "Feel like obeying God, feel like doing the right thing." Argh!! I can't find a place in the Bible where God says to feel like doing anything! Like the sports ad say, "Just do it!" God says the good feelings will come. Is it, "Memorize two scriptures and call me in the morning?"

No, sometimes I think we want to manipulate God and say, "I found a magic formula in scripture, and if I do this (whatever this is), God will do such and such for me." We cannot force God to do anything. We must join God's Anonymous. I am powerless over God. God's not some little genie in a bottle, who jumps when I rub the lantern. God is so much more different than I can ever imagine. Even in Heaven, I won't be on a par with God. God wants me to love and obey Him out of love, not because I expect Him to put out or come through in some way. This is not a contract, that at some specific time God will grant me the goodies. God calls me to faithfulness, God gives good things to "the just and the unjust." Does God love believers in Africa any less, when they are persecuted, murdered or sold into slavery (Yes, this is true in 2004.) Does God love me more, because I have a vehicle, a place to live, a job that provides enough for food and clothing? Do I have more faith? Do they have less faith? The point is, God wants me dependent on Him, no matter what the circumstances. This is success. Proverbs 30:8-9 (NIV), .".give me neither poverty nor riches, but give me only my daily bread. Otherwise, I may have too much and disown you and say, 'Who is the Lord?' Or I may become poor and steal, and so dishonour the name of my God." Gratitude is Godliness. "I've learned by now to be quite content whatever my circumstances," Philippians 4:11.

Forgiveness is the other major thing I wish weren't presented in Scripture, the way it is. The Lord's Prayer, Our Father (Vater unser) says, "forgive us as we forgive." No! I don't want that. I want to be forgiven. I want those whom I'm angry at to get judgment, like some of the Psalms talk about: "Fry 'em, Nuke 'em, Roast 'em!" I'm glad God didn't strike me with lightning when I sinned. Lord knows, I'd have been toast years ago. I forgive, because it's right and because I want to be forgiven. Forgiveness is a choice - it's a gift I give myself. When I don't forgive, I'm the one who carries resentment and bitterness - I become a sour, bitter, resentful person who blames others and feels like a victim. Do you want to be around me when I'm that kind of person? I seriously doubt it. When I love God and myself, I will want to forgive you. I don't have to go tell you or others - that can be a subtle way or not so subtle way of knifing you. I have given up my "right" to punish you. I do this at a specific time and I may need to do this one day at a time, many times. Yes, I can tell you, if you decide to come to me to talk about the specific situation.

This situation is called: reconciliation (this is how we can become friends again, we settle the score, not by getting even). There is a big difference between forgiveness and reconciliation. I can decide to forgive. I cannot decide that we will reconcile. Reconciliation takes two willing parties: the offended and the offender. Let us say I offended you. I did something that violated you in some way. It makes no difference what it is or was. My first step is to come and confess my offense (perhaps an apology). I own or admit what I did or didn't do (said or didn't say). I don't talk about what you did or didn't say/do, only about my responsibility. The words "but" or "if only you" or anything similar, never appear, or there is no valid confession. These words wipe out an apology and reconciliation is not possible at this point. When my ego gets hooked in this way, I want to excuse my behavior and make you responsible or blame you. I may need to write this out beforehand, read it outloud to myself or others (this makes it more real, and a good friend will call me on any games I am trying to play).

Once I am able to confess, then another important word comes into play: repentance. When I repent, I turn from the wrong behavior or thinking and turn to new, right behavior. The reconciliation may still not be possible, because at this point my words may only be words, and you may not have a track record to look at and actually know that my actions match my words (talk the talk and walk the walk, in AA terms). Being able to hold this ambiguity, not having things settled yet, without letting my anxiety about this tension lead me to further inappropriate behavior is not easy. I could sit there, drumming my fingers impatiently, waiting for you to "kiss and make up." Again, success here is my confession and repentance, not your willingness to reconcile. I am powerless over you. Impatience will sabotage the process and puts idolatry in place.

I have seen couples with far greater difficulties between them, reconcile. I have seen couples with relatively fewer issues, divorce. No matter what, success is me being who God has called me to be. God didn't go on vacation and put me in charge of convicting anyone else of their sins. "Father, forgive me, for I know not what I do."

I have begun thinking about life as follows: When a thought comes to mind, I ask myself, "Is God telling me this or Satan?" I would wager that 99% of situations are very easy to figure out. The other 1% can wait for God to let me know, I don't have to do anything with these exceptions for now.

CHAPTER 7

"Brevity is next to Godliness"

O k, somebody said, "cleanliness is next to Godliness," where does brevity come from? Well, "When words are many, sin is not absent." (Proverbs 10:19, NIV) Brevity means being succinct, brief or concise in my speaking. Believe me, writing this book is challenging my desire to say less. Here I will put anything I believe is helpful, which I was not able to fit in other chapters.

I own nothing. Right, yes I have a vehicle and furniture, etc. I won't take it with me. My children may not want anything I have. When I begin to understand that I came into this world with nothing and will leave with nothing, I begin to be able to understand what is important. I will not die with an empty in-box. There will always be something good I could have done. If I do all the good things, I may not have time to do the best. The only things I can count on is change and suffering. I am a servant and should expect to suffer as Jesus suffered. Life is not about pain reduction. It's about staying in relationship with God while I experience life's pain. I want to enjoy life and God says if I serve Him, I will have what I need and can enjoy life with Him now and in the life to come. This world is not my home - I am simply passing through.

I believe we encounter something in life, where we feel like we're being dangled over the Grand Canyon, without a safety net or bungee cord. This is a point where I feel fear or disappointment so intensely, that I vow to never feel that amount of pain or hurt ever again. This is something I may remember, most of the time I believe it is a saved file, as well as stored in our body. As I stand a ways from the Grand Canyon, suddenly I see someone I would like to get close to on the other side of the canyon. I begin to move in that direction and run splat into an invisible plexiglass barrier, where my heart or body lets me know, "No way!" We swore an oath we would never get close enough to someone again, where we would risk this kind of injury, pain or disappointment again. It could be losing a parent or feeling rejected. It's much like a plant that grows in some direction, where a shoot or tendril experiences trauma and stops growing in that direction. If enough damage occurs, the plant may not grow in any direction. It may simply exist. I can be like that plant. Existence or comfortable numbness may seem safer, more preferable, to risking. "The hell I know may feel safer, than the heaven you promise." The unknown can seem scarier than the known. Living can seem like a bigger risk than simply staying in my Hobbit hole. An adventure can seem like a fate worse than death.

How can I be free from these shackles or constraints? "But I need something more! For if I know the law but still can't keep it, and if the power of sin within me keeps sabotaging my best intentions, I obviously need help! I realize that I don't have what it takes. I can will it, but I can't do it. I decide to do good, but I don't really do it; I decide not to do bad, but then I do it anyway. My decisions, such as they are, don't result in actions. Something has gone wrong deep within me and gets the better of me every time." (Romans 7:17-20) I can identify with this. Part of what can happen in therapy is becoming open and feeling safe and walking through this valley of the shadow of death. This is not an easy journey (process again). Adventure provides an opportunity to develop strength and discover the strength and tenacity God has given me. Without the opportunity, I'm a race horse stuck in the stable with hobbles. Since God didn't give me a spirit of fear, I know where my fear comes from. I risk. I may not feel like risking and I want to be free to live with my identity in Christ. I talk about my fears in my relationship with my therapist or a close friend who is able to be objective (not an easy task - there's a reason therapists aren't ethically supposed to do therapy with family members or friends). A therapist is not designed to be your friend, or anything more intimate than even friendship. This is also not an easy process financially, in this day of managed care (cost). It is worth it. You are worth it. Yes, it is more than words. It is empathy, not sympathy. To develop relationship with God or another person we learn to walk a mile in their shoes, boots or moccasins. God already did that for us.

How do I develop this intimacy? There are so many resources. John Eldredge has written helpful books and there are many others. Intimacy is knowing myself and another. I can't expose your cards and you can't reveal mine. I do this freely because I long for relationship. I talk to God. Certainly God can read my mind and He wants me to talk, that's how relationship develops. It takes time and interaction. Quantity time provides the setting for quality time. I can't schedule quality time. I tell God what's going on in me. I pray for God to change me. I don't focus on you. I can pray for you. My prayer for you is, "God do whatever You want to do in his or her life, to make them the man or woman You want them to be." This is the prayer I heard as a teenager, walking in on my parents, when I was under the influence of alcohol or drugs and threatened to kill my parents. "And please don't let him hurt anyone else in the process." God answered that prayer and I hope He answers your prayer. Prayer works better than nagging - then I'm not a nag.

My problem with prayer, is my desire to tell God how to bring about change in my life. I really want to tell Him how to bring about change in your life. Since joining God's Anonymous, I realize I need to leave things in His hands. He works very efficiently and in His ways. I tend to want to get my little toy toolbox and get my plastic hammer, saw and screwdriver. "Alright, God. I've got this under control. If I need a little assistance or advice, I'll ask you." I visualize God sitting behind the wheel of a humongous 18-wheeler, semi-truck, yawning and saying, "Well, alright, I'll just take a nap here, since you think you have it all under control. When you're ready, I'll get out my super-professional quality tools, which this truck is full of. Oh, by the way, remember that my natural laws are still in place. The person you're trying to control and fix would have some natural consequences and other stuff falling on them. Since you've put yourself in between them and Me, don't be surprised when stuff happens, to you."

As I learn to let God be in charge, and learn to deal with the 2x4 in my own eye, I tend to hit people less in the head with my board. I don't see as clearly anyhow, so my little tweezer doesn't help me trying to get the splinter out of someone's eye. I learn to judge others less, and trust that most people are like I am. I want to pretty much do the right thing. I want to love and be loved. I want to know how to love, be loved and do the right thing. Change brings hope and with hope comes joy (which does not depend on my circumstances - happiness tends to be based on my situation).

"It is more blessed to give than to receive" (Acts 20:35, KJV). God talks a lot about giving and receiving. I have seen this facet of truth put together with "Owe no man anything" (Romans 13:8, KJV) in an interesting way. The conclusion I have heard stated and seen in effect is this: Since it's more blessed to give than to receive and I should owe no one anything, I should give and not receive. If I receive, then I owe and that will be hanging over my head - they will have a claim on me. Plus, if I give, then I'm ok. If I'm receiving, I'm needy, dependent and not taking care of myself. I am vulnerable and I don't want to be or feel vulnerable. I should be able to pull myself up by my own bootstraps. Check in with your belief and thought system and see what you say when you feel needy or someone wants to give to you. I'd rather stop and render aid, than be the one who needs aid. There can be a subtle pride in this. What has also made sense to clients, is this: "I want to hog all the blessings, by doing all the giving." When I am able to receive, I give others the opportunity to receive a blessing. I can bless others by needing. There's a yucky feel to a relationship that is one-sided. I believe relationships are best, when there is mutual, reciprocal giving and receiving.

"Our Father, who art in Heaven....." Here is an unfortunate reality: we tend to experience God, or see God, project onto God our experience with our earthly parents. No, it's not fair to God or myself. As I begin to learn to choose my thoughts and beliefs, I can free myself to learn to know God as God, rather than creating God in my image, or that of my biological or earthly father or mother. Certainly I don't change who God is - yup, God's Anonymous again - however, just as I am limited in my using the computer I'm using, because to me it's just a fancy, modern typewriter I can also send letters with, if there's a proper connection available - my ignorance about God limits my relationship with Him. This computer can do far and above what I am able to imagine, my understanding and belief affects me, not the computer.

An important part of learning about my body, mind and spirituality is learning to integrate all of me. As a Christian, this means I give up compartmentalizing the different parts of me. Envision a post office, where there are many mailboxes. In many of these, I have placed different parts of myself. What I do different days of the week, how I am at work, how I am at home, with friends, what I think about and so forth. Somewhere around the point of diminishing returns, these mailboxes start opening on their own. I am running around and trying to slam the little doors shut, spinning the dials, to keep the different parts of myself locked away. I've told one person one thing, another a different part of myself. It's not working anymore. It's time for me to go to God with all of me and to accept myself, so I don't think I still need to hide. Life is matching meaning to my behavior.

Nothing, unless I reject God and/or kill myself, is a show-stopper. I can change my thoughts, beliefs and behaviors. Before I explore myself, become aware of my thoughts and beliefs, I don't change. I may be disappointed and give up - resigning myself to self-pity, where I believe I will never get needs met. I tend to believe I'm not worthy. In Aesop's fables, the fox is not able to reach the grapes and decides to believe they are sour and I wouldn't want them anyhow. This non sequitur leads me to give up and not even try, because trying the same things over and over again didn't change anyone else and get me what I wanted. The other extreme I can go to is demanding what I want and forcing others to do or give. I may get something and it's not from the heart. It will be empty, because I thought I deserved something and intimidated others. An in between place is where I still desire something, am able to feel my disappointment and not think or believe it's the end of the world. I call this a place of emotional integrity. I am alive, rather than existing. In the place of resignation, I can be trying to avoid feeling, because I decide I won't want or ask, so I don't feel disappointment. Here I am existing. In the demand place, I'm also trying to control my feelings, because I believe if I don't get what I want, I will feel overwhelmed by what I feel.

A whole different place is that of adolescent integrity. Here, I set up life to resist change and resist becoming an adult. I am recalcitrant (being obstinate, defiant, not cooperating).

An adolescent can detect hypocrisy a mile away, and does not want to be fake. This can be an admirable attribute. An adolescent can tell if I'm wearing a shirt that says, "Take my advice, I'm not using it!" The adolescent integrity also has a less desirable side. This doesn't necessarily go away with age, unless I change my thinking. I'm told most guys, and perhaps gals, today don't get out of adolescence before age 30. When I see an older person, I can generally tell whether their thinking and attitude has been positive or negative. Since practice makes better, what I've been practicing will show. If I've been a generally happy person, you can see it. If I've been negative, you also will probably be able to see how I've been soaking in vinegar.

The down side to adolescent integrity is when someone tells me to do something, I do the opposite, because "I'm gonna show you who's the boss." If you tell me to go left, I go right. If you tell me to go up, I say .... well, I won't write what an adolescent usually says, or acts out. The ironic part of this is, by reacting to others, I'm giving them power over me. I gain agency, power in my own life, when I know what I want to do and then do it, whether mom and dad think that's also the thing I should do. If someone tells me to not do something, and I don't think I should do it either, I would be shooting myself in the foot, cutting off my nose to spite my face, if I did something just because someone told me not to. Part of being an adult is doing what I know to be right, whether it's fun or not. Doing or not doing what I believe, whether it's easy or not. Then I stop giving others power over me, and successfully perform surgery on the umbilical cord. I don't cut the apron strings by moving or pursuing a lifestyle that's opposed to what God or my parents or boss or ex or whoever thinks I should do. You may remember the telephone ad, "Long distance, the next best thing to being there."

Long distance can also be the next worst thing to being there. I can give others power over me over the phone. I don't even need the phone or email - I usually have internalized the voices I react to, until I exorcise them. When I'm wearing the shirt that says, "Take my advice - I'm not using it" an adolescent will pick up on this.

I may also need a t-shirt that says, "I'm not your dad" or "I'm not your mom" or "I'm not my dad" or "I'm not my mom." It is easy to project that someone is like a person from my past, especially when I haven't resolved my issues with that person. It can be confusing, because I can relate to someone in a way that invites them to treat me the way I'm used to being treated. If I haven't worked through the issues - I may not be able to see behavior that is different from what I'm used to. I still see what I see, rather than what is truly there. Remember, it takes time to adjust. I can see this more clearly when I know I've changed, and someone still relates to me as I used to be. My first impression can take time to change. "Use it or lose it!" As you develop a pattern of change, you will retain more of this change. "Don't use it and lost it!" As I no longer have a pattern of old unhelpful words, thoughts or behaviors, I will slowly lose them.

Clients and others ask me what I think about dreams. I think God gives us dreams to let us know something we're ready to deal with. Certainly Daniel and Joseph dealt with dreams. God gave them wisdom. I don't have the hubris (arrogance or negative pride) to think I'm on their level. I view dreams as follows: Remember all those files inside of us? Well, there are many more. Surgeons tell us when they touch a specific area of the brain, patients remember things they had forgotten. Our brain has more memory than we can normally access. This is why I offered the web exercise. When I am on screen-saver (asleep or dozing), my computer says, "What information did we take in today? Let's file it. As files are opened to see what needs to be done in that file, because of information I took in today, God lets information come up, out of the files. This is information God knows I'm ready to deal with, whether I agree I'm ready to deal with it or not. This is not a printout, with 10 points all in order. The memories I have are from different times in my life. The images represent the issue or memory I'm ready to deal with.

Some people take a book that purports (claims) to say what different symbols or images represent. I don't look at dreams in this way. My experience, based on Jungian teaching, has shown me that I or a book can't tell you what an image means to you.

If I ask you what a corn cob means to you, you may think of hogs, corn on the cob, brewing, the Thanksgiving Day cornucopia or the Nebraska Cornhuskers. A snake means different things to different people. So, I don't go to a book, I ask you what the images, colors, people, objects or anything else in your dream means to you. By working through these images, we arrive at a place where you are able to receive information you can use. Certainly there are reports of inventions being discovered through dreams. I think they're very powerful and have never heard or had a dream I would call wierd. Someone who doesn't understand the nature of dreams might be embarassed or ashamed. To me, dreams rarely mean what they appear to on the surface. To me they're normal, if we are able to get good sleep. Nightmares are another matter, which can come from trauma - still need to be looked at - or from medicine side effects or other medical conditions. I feel honored when someone trusts me enough to share a dream. One thing I tell people, if they want to dream and remember dreams, is this: keep pen and paper next to your bed and write everything down as soon as you are able. It can help to set your alarm clock a couple minutes earlier, which can have you at that place where dreams have not faded away. If you don't remember, God will let you know again. Before you go to sleep, ask God to show you, give Him and yourself permission to dream.

I want to briefly talk about some more male-female differences. The part of this, for much has been written, I want to emphasize is: emotionally there are great differences. Two wonderful resources are "What Could He Be Thinking" by Michael Gurian (certainly parts come from a non-Christian perspective); and "Bringing Up Boys" by James Dobson. I preface this with again saying men and women can learn to be bilingual, to where they can understand each other, without needing to criticize the differences. Women's brains have more and larger areas dedicated to words and feelings, than men do. Women's brain get 15% more blood flow, than men's brains. You have probably experienced a woman being able to say what she thinks more quickly than a man. He searches for the right words. Researchers hid microphones on playgrounds and found that girls talked about feelings and relationships, while boys tended to make sounds or use less complex words, certainly not about relationships. When we accept the differences and don't expect males to be females or females to be males, life works so much better. It helps to get the perspective of the gender I'm dealing with.

Dr. Carol Lewis, M.D. (psychiatrist at my office) aptly says, "Women don't understand what it's like for men to live under the influence of testosterone." I would equally say, "Men don't have a clue what it's like for women to live under the influence of estrogen, nor what it's like for women, living with a man's testosterone." Wanting to understand helps celebrate the full breadth of life.

Another difference I've seen: A woman is talking to a man and watches him for cues that he's getting it - he understands. If she doesn't see something that to her says "He understands," and she doesn't ask, "What do you hear me saying?," she will tend to either say the exact same thing or say it differently, trying to get her message across. When a man hears a woman, he needs to tell her, "I got it - and here's what I heard." Otherwise, both get frustrated and he tends to tune her out and who knows where this will end up. Both are responsible for themselves, and can be bilingual and learn to understand the other.

To me, men and women are like a car's headlights: can we survive a drive with only the left or only the right headlights? Often we can. We see more and are probably going to be safer with both. I don't care which one is left or right, my point is: men see the world differently than a woman does. A further difference in the male brain takes place during the second trimester of gestation: a testosterone wash goes over the male fetus' brain and separates many of the synapses or connecters of the two sides of the brain. Yes, we men know women often think we're brain damaged. It's sort of true. Women tend to come into the world able to see or perceive the world with both parts of their brain. Men tend to see the world from one side of the brain. A man asks a woman for input, and when she doesn't give him a list with the logical reasons for what she thinks, tends to discount her until he learns about the differences and becomes bilingual. She can see things in a way he is not able. We need both in marriage. Accept the difference. She needs him, he needs her.

Gary Chapman, the author of "The Five Love Languages," gives us a great gift. We each have different needs. Different things ring my chimes than yours. When I get to know myself, I can ask for what I want, and feel loved. This is adult. You can find out what speaks love to you and ask for it. Write out what actions your partner does which speak love to you. I can write out what I'm doing that to me says, "I love you." I may be sincere in what I'm doing, and if it doesn't speak that to you, I can change. My adolescent integrity can stubbornly say, "Well, I'm showing you and if you don't accept it - Tough!" This will continue getting what I've gotten up till now. Just doing what I want to or "That's how I feel!," is not love - it's selfishness. Different currencies ring different cash registers. I can tell you a lot in German and if you don't understand German, my words, thoughts and feelings, won't mean a thing to you, no matter how sincere I am. If I want to love and be loved - I can change. I can see that what you are doing or saying is either expressing love or asking for love - yes, I can learn to be bilingual. I believe most of us are doing the best we can, and with the grace of God, I can become more complete. I don't have to judge you, because then - I'm asking for the same level of judgment. We all make mistakes - we all need God's forgiveness, grace and mercy.

I also don't have to criticize how you worship. Religion can be the opiate of the people, especially when we're out of balance. You may worship with different kinds of songs or music; with or without instruments. If you are worshipping God - hallelujah! Every body of worship needs people gifted with different gifts, that's why God gave them. If I say my gift is better than the one of another church or whatever, I'm in hubris - arrogance - and can fall on my knees and say, "God, be merciful to me - a sinner."

Sometimes, to help clients access memories or healing, I ask them to do the following exercise. If they have an issue with someone, I ask them to write this person a letter they don't send, with their dominant hand (if you're right-handed you write with your right hand - if you're left-handed you write with your left hand). Then I ask them to let the other person write back with the non-dominant hand. Feel free to try this and don't analyze or think about this too much. Just let it happen. This allows us to access the other hemisphere or other side of our brain. This can be very powerful and helpful.

I always prefer any writing to be done by hand and not on a computer, because we slow down and are more conscious about what we're writing. When my body and hand are more involved, something very different happens, than when I'm speeding along on a keyboard. Also, in this age of computers, anything you write on a computer, whether you drag it off to the trash or not can be recovered. You privacy is of utmost importance to me. In addition, having testified in court on numerous occasions, I know that things we write may be "discoverable." I don't usually keep things clients write, and a ceremony of burning written things and scattering or burying the ashes can be therapeutic.

Prayer and forgiveness and renewing my mind change me. Awareness helps me come to a place where I can change. The book of James talks about looking in a mirror, gaining the insight is useful, unless it is simply knowledge. When I change, knowledge changes into wisdom. Mere knowledge brings arrogance.

Look at your calendar and checkbook (what you spend your money on) - this will tell you what you have valued and what your higher power has been up till now. As is true with any trip with a car, I may have been headed in some direction, and now that I'm deciding to go another direction, I can take the next exit and go in a new direction, no matter what plan I've had so far.

I want to go back to the honey and vinegar. It is honest, and perhaps sometimes helpful to say what I don't want, and how I feel about not getting what I want. I believe there is a further step. Once I am able to be aware of what I want and don't want and am able to begin asking for what I want, a further adjustment is possible. The fine tuning is this: I will invite getting more of what I want, when I ask for what I want. The previous first step was to say: "When you...... (do/don't do - say, don't say) I feel........ (glad, sad, mad, afraid or shame - the most basic feelings). When a relationship can tolerate this kind of communication, it has come a long way. Asking in the positive, improves my odds of receiving more of what I want. "When you this (positive behavior or word(s), I feel.....(positive feeling). It works - believe me. This is similar to research that says when I say "remember this," another person will more likely remember and do, rather than saying "don't forget to....."

There are a lot of questions and awareness available, which is what I've written about. I'd prefer you don't overanalyze everything - at the same time, if you're reading this, you probably want to change something in your life, so you are going to analyze things more for a while. The goal is to become more aware, so you can decide what you want to change. Since it is a process, you may write down your new beliefs and put them on cards to carry around with you, or on sticky notes. I suggest you don't put them on your car dashboard - there's enough to be aware of when we're driving, with three mirrors usually and everything else. I want your safety. The writing down, however you decide to do it, is to relearn. As my father often said, "Repetition is the mother of all learning." When I want to eat something, buy something, go to an entertainment place, be with another person, I can ask my self, "What am I feeling? What is the emotion I'm eating or drinking, What is the emotion I'm trying to buy?." This is living consciously rather than letting my past, my old tapes/self-talk or thoughts and my reactions from any other time than now controlling my life.

I cannot over-emphasize enough, "expect an adjustment period to change." Here is what can happen. If I decide to move away from my family of origin, family members may be upset with me. If I change churches, someone may be upset with me. When people change and no longer let their addictions control their lives, others adjust or don't. In twelve-step groups, we learn we may need to decide to change who we hang out with. Those I've hung out with, up till now, may have the same stinking thinkin I've had. We tend to adopt the values and behaviors and thinking of those we hang out with. That's no surprize. Read Proverbs, look at gangs, crowds we hung out with growing up, cliques - we often speak of mob mentality, group think, crowd behavior - as my father often said, "If you play with a skunk, you'll smell like a skunk." Others may not be comfortable with how I now think, act or believe. Maybe I'm learning new things to enjoy and old ways no longer bring joy, rather, since I'm living consciously (thinking for my self with God's help) I know my values are more in agreement, more in concert, with God's. My family of choice, is always a choice, and as I change, I may need to go through a grieving process as I move to a new place. I can't control how others feel - I also don't need to be a jerk about it. I make it about me - "I don't enjoy this behavior" rather than "You're stupid for wanting to do that." I don't have to label or define others. I can leave the door open for them to ask me why I'm different, why the 2x4 in my eye is now down to a 1x4. "When I was a child, I talked like a child, I thought like a child, I reasoned like a child. When I became a man, I put childish ways behind me." (I Corinthians 13: 11, NIV)

I don't beat up myself for how I've thought in the past. I recognize and move on. This is the difference between Simon Peter, who denied he knew Jesus three times; and Judas Iscariot, who betrayed Jesus. Peter grieved and moved on - God used Peter mightily. Judas beat up himself and hanged himself - God was not able to use Judas, because Judas was dead. "I am growing up now" is more helpful than, "I've been such a dummy." Now I learn to think as God would have me think - not the pack instinct as at sporting events or when an armored car loses cash on the street. I don't have to take my cues for my behavior from others and stop thinking - I get into my neo-cortex and put myself less in situations where in the past I have given up my own agency. I may be able to be strong later, now I'm in training. Whatever my downfall, I don't have to put myself in a place of temptation - I can resist and flee. What others think about my not staying in that situation, I have no control over.

Ceremonies are important in a society: baptisms/christenings/-dedications, bar mitzvahs/communions/confirmations, weddings, graduations and funerals. The ceremony I believe we can help ourselves with is akin to the bachelor/bachelorette party, before a wedding. I'm not suggesting going drinking and other sexual activities some may participate in - the concept is about moving from one phase of life to the next stage (you know, how parents mourn when the kids are all out of the house and out of college and on their own, making their own money and paying their own bills). Make a ceremony for yourself with the changes you're making from your old way of thinking, to the new way you are learning. Celebrate with trusted friends, or do it on your own or both. Hallelujah!

Learning to respond, rather than react, is so freeing. Otherwise, when I experience someone as being critical of me, I tend to react out of that adolescent "integrity" place, where I either "tell someone where to go," withdraw or try to please them. Since I want to be more in charge of my actions, when I am aware that I'm experiencing someone as critical, I let myself know that if I don't decide to do things differently, I will react as in the past. Equally, if I experience someone in that adolescent "integrity" place: rebellious, trying to kiss up or isolating; my default mode will be to become critical - parental, pedantic or condescending. I can never control how someone else experiences me and I can control myself and respond. I don't need to go to someone and tell them how I experience them. I just know I want to change the yucky games I've been stuck in up till now.

Some years ago, I was doing my annual "going bowling for an hour or two." As I was bowling, someone came up behind me and said, "Move over to your right a few boards." I didn't react internally or externally, I just accepted his suggestion. After a few more frames, he said, "Crouch lower." Ok, I did it. Then he said, "Hold your arm/hand straight." I bowled a few more frames and turned around - he was gone. I consciously thought about the things he'd told me and initially my score was lower. Then, all of a sudden, my score started going way up, as I no longer needed to think about it - I was unconsciously doing what I had learned. As I checked out of the bowling alley, I asked about him, and discovered this man was a former pro bowler.

"Beauty is in the eye of the beholder." We've all heard this. It is true and not true. The truth is: If I think you are beautiful (or anything else), then to me you are. No matter what you think. If you think you are beautiful, then you are - no matter what I think. If you think you're ugly, then it doesn't matter what I think - you will not be able to take in how I see you. Learning to think differently, initially being able to say, "It's hard for me to take in your compliment or gratitude or view of me," rather than "You're crazy" or "You're full of it" or "There's something wrong with you, if you see me as beautiful" or "What is she or he up to?," or "If you only knew the real me"(of course, I'm not going to let you see the real me, because I fear what you'll do - so I'm guaranteed not feeling loved because I won't give you a chance), or "I really pulled the wool over your eyes). Please read Lori Heyman Gordon - "Love Knots." When I am not able to take in your positive view of me, it will be difficult for me to respond back positively, until I learn to accept myself and love myself. During my learning curve, I can put my hand on my heart, breathe, feel my feet and say, "I want to take in your compliment. Thank you." "Thank you," is the best possible response, rather than "It's no big deal." This is a similar issue in French, "de rien" (it's nothing), the same in Spanish "de nada" or German "macht nichts" or "keine Ursache."

A word about pornography and romance novels: I find both of these damaging to healthy relationships. Both objectify and abuse women, as well as men. They encourage a living in fantasy, where he always knows what she wants, without her needing to ask. He's available, has resources very few have. It's a setup, an escape and addictive. Pornography is even more insidious (dangerous and treacherous). Our minds are a battle place, where Satan wants to cripple us and take us out of combat. Life is combat - expect it. Sexual sin is listed in sentences with overeating, gossip, lying, murder, etc. Sin is sin! And sexual sin is also very different, whether it's in our minds or we act it out physically. We are joined with another person through the sexual act or fantasy, and then we aren't as available to a real person, where the daily living is not always a fantasy, rather sometimes a nightmare. Fred Stoeker and Stephen Arterburn's, "Every Man's Battle" is a great resource as is "Every Woman's Battle" by Shannon Ethridge and Stephen Arterburn.

Today, I am who I am and where I am. I cannot do anything about my past. I confess any past sin, and don't use any past decisions, to justify future sin or faulty decisions. You may say, "We got married for the wrong reason(s)." I'm not sure many of us do get married for totally adult and spiritual reasons. Listening to my heart, apart from God and my mind and grown-up parts is not wise. Whatever the situation, now I am where I am. Now I can make a Godly decision. While if I sin more, I can receive more grace and mercy, God doesn't want me to test Him in that way. Somebody else does. What does God want me to learn in my situation? As Job said, "Because even if he killed me, I'd keep on hoping." (Job 13:15) Shadrach, Meshach, and Abednego said, "If you throw us in the fire, the God we serve can rescue us .....But even if he doesn't....We still wouldn't serve your gods...." (Daniel 3:16-18) Look to God because you love Him and want a relationship with Him - not as your lucky rabbit's foot, insurance policy or SWAT team. I want as much pain avoidance as the next person and God will walk through my Death Valley with me.

I want intimacy and partnership. I think we all would say the same thing. Everything I've written about is designed to show how I can have a healthy interdependent life. I can learn how I've thought, believed, felt and acted in ways that have kept me either dependent or independent. Independence, "I did it my way," is part of what the world is wanting to teach me - it's the original sin. Adam and Eve both did this. We have all learned too well - "God, you're not coming through for me - you're holding out on me - so I'll take matters in my own hands and make my decisions apart from your will." If God says, "Don't lie or steal or covet or rob a bank or commit adultery, I don't need to pray and seek God's will in matters which are very clear. A true statement here can be: Instead of "I don't love you," "I'm not acting lovingly toward you and I believe I should feel a certain way before I can act lovingly." Adam chose Eve over God. Eve became Adam's higher power - this was idolatry, just like knowledge became Eve's higher power. We men have sought woman to make us happy, make us feel loved or make us feel like a man. Nobody can make me anything. We men have tended to either squash women, because we're angry she hasn't validated us as a man, or tried to kiss up to her and please her (act nice, when we're actually angry) to get what we want. Neither extreme is healthy. The greatest commandment is to love God, then neighbor. When I seek His kingdom and righteousness, then the other things can fall into place.

A current and centuries long problem which shows the principles of this book is the Arab-Jewish conflict. What one generation has passed on to the next, has continued beliefs about the other side. For decades some Arabs and Jews have attempted to learn to understand each other and talk with each other. Again, we have no control over others. Some extremists have been unhappy with the possibility of positive understanding, and some seeking to gain understanding have paid with their lives. Change is never easy and I have no control over others.

EPILOGUE

My hope and prayer is that you would find more wholeness. I have enjoyed this hard, arduous writing process. My writing days have been 10-16 hour days, periodically interrupted by someone calling to talk about a situation in their life, another asking about a dream, the monthly exterminator, a pizza delivery I didn't order and didn't try to rescue the pizza guy from his frustration. I walked in the rain (yes, I picked up lots of aluminum cans), swam, made some calls about authors and books and spellings. I ate healthfully - except for the chocolate bar yesterday, which really affected me and knocked me out - I hadn't had sugar in a long time. My process also was not pure writing - how can I separate what I've written and just compartmentalize it? I'm glad to be done - still have some computer related program things to do. Thank you Timothy Ko, colleage, author and computer guru at work. Thank you Lord. I enjoyed the time alone and am ready to be back with family.

Post script:

God has a sense of humor. This book just flowed. I had written notes and did refer to them on occasion. I checked a few things in the "Baker Encyclopedia of Psychology," edited by David G. Benner (a wonderful resource). I had my unabridged Websters dictionary to check my spelling (yes, I prefer hands on, I like to go into the bank, see a real cashier at the store). Here's what's ironic. I finally went out to drive the island, I didn't realize how big it is. I had thought I could easily walk it. As I drove I heard a song that went something like this: "It only hurts when I breathe, so I hold my breath so I don't feel." Pain avoidance to not feel and then not working through the old files. Our society teaches us to hold our breath, suck in the stomach, all of which makes it harder to breathe and feel. Many a country song speaks of using alcohol or another lover to get over the previous one - anything...and then the pain when I do it to myself all over again. Ouch! Here's the ironic part - my colleagues, there are some 20+ therapists at our center, know I haven't really touched on my greatest passion. It only came to me on the drive. I was sure I had pretty much written everything I wanted to and it might take another decade for another book. Hmmm.

CPSIA information can be obtained
at www.ICGtesting.com
Printed in the USA
LVHW042355190619
621814LV00002B/249

9 781594 67679